No Child Left Behind

PRIMER

PETER LANG
New York • Washington, D.C./Baltimore • Bern
Frankfurt am Main • Berlin • Brussels • Vienna • Oxford

Frederick M. Hess
Michael J. Petrilli

No Child Left Behind
PRIMER

PETER LANG
New York • Washington, D.C./Baltimore • Bern
Frankfurt am Main • Berlin • Brussels • Vienna • Oxford

Library of Congress Cataloging-in-Publication Data
Hess, Frederick M..
No Child Left Behind primer / Frederick M. Hess, Michael J. Petrilli
p. cm.
Includes bibliographical references.
1. United States. No Child Left Behind Act of 2001. 2. Educational
accountability— Law and legislation— United States. 3. School improvement
programs— United States. I. Petrilli, Michael J. II. Title.
KF4125.Z9H47 2006   379.1'580973— dc22   2006000066
ISBN 0-8204-7844-X

Bibliographic information published by **Die Deutsche Bibliothek.**
Die Deutsche Bibliothek lists this publication in the "Deutsche
Nationalbibliografie"; detailed bibliographic data is available
on the Internet at http://dnb.ddb.de/.

The authors would like to thank a number of individuals for their
assistance with this project. We particularly want to thank Andrew
Kelly and Morgan Goatley for their invaluable help in researching
and preparing the manuscript, and Sara Mead for her work on
chapter 4. We would also like to thank Juliet Squire, Michael
Ruderman, Erin Riley, and Rich Gioia for their assistance with
research and manuscript preparation, and Tom Corwin for his
guidance and thoughtful suggestions. We'd also like to
acknowledge the American Enterprise Institute and the
Thomas B. Fordham Foundation for the support and institutional
resources necessary to support this endeavor. We would also like
to express our appreciation to Chris Myers, the Managing Director,
and to Lisa Dillon, Production/Creative Director of Peter Lang
Publishing. Finally, we are indebted to Joleen and Meghan
for all their love and support.

The paper in this book meets the guidelines for permanence and durability
of the Committee on Production Guidelines for Book Longevity
of the Council of Library Resources.

© 2006 Peter Lang Publishing, Inc., New York
29 Broadway, New York, NY 10006
www.peterlang.com

Printed in the United States of America

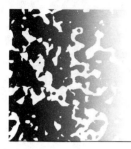

Table of Contents

Introduction 1

1   The Background of NCLB 3

2   NCLB Testing, Accountability, and Choice 27

3   The Highly Qualified Teacher Provision 63

4   Other Major Programs and Policies 93

5   Politics, Implementation, and Future Challenges 119

     Appendix: The Many Programs of NCLB 135

     Notes 141

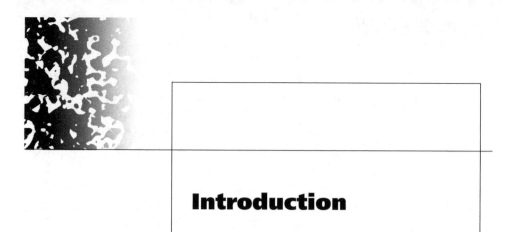

Introduction

This volume considers the key elements of the No Child Left Behind Act of 2001 (NCLB), how they are intended to work, how they are being implemented, and the law's prospects. We do not attempt to assess the merits of NCLB, to evaluate whether the law has been "successful," or to provide recommendations. This book is for people who want to understand the law, not for people who are seeking a defense, a critique, or an evaluation. With that, let us briefly explain how this primer will unfold.

In chapter 1, we provide a history of the No Child Left Behind Act. We explain the law's origins and logic, why it is structured the way it is, and the concerns of its critics.

In chapter 2, we examine the central innovation of NCLB—its ambitious assessment and accountability system. We explain the testing provisions that states are required to implement, how the accountability system is designed to work, the law's requirements for schools and school districts that fail to make adequate progress, and the options to be provided to the parents of children in these schools.

In chapter 3, we discuss the law's mandate that, by 2006, every child be taught by a "highly qualified teacher." We briefly explain the larger debate on teacher quality, discuss how the law defines "highly qualified," and review how states have sought to address the challenge.

While the accountability and highly qualified teacher provisions are the most significant and controversial elements of NCLB, they constitute only a small portion of the sprawling law. In chapter 4, we consider other key provisions—including the law's strong language calling for expanded use of "scientifically based research," especially as it relates to the Reading First program. In this chapter, we also discuss the question of whether NCLB is adequately funded. Finally, while most of the law's other provisions are programs inherited from earlier versions of the Elementary and Secondary Education Act (ESEA), some were modified in important ways. Even those that remain unchanged may be unfamiliar to many readers, so we explain them here.

Finally, in chapter 5, we discuss the implementation and political challenges facing the law and offer some thoughts as to the political support that may be necessary if the law is to fulfill its creators' aspirations. No Child Left Behind is probably the most ambitious and far-reaching education legislation that Congress has ever passed. Its aims are far more dramatic than those of the original Elementary and Secondary Education Act, and it calls for a federal role that is far more active than that envisioned by ESEA. Whether NCLB is a "good law" and whether it is working as intended are questions about which reasonable observers will disagree. Our aim is to explain the law more fully, outline its features, and explain its implementation so that you, the reader, can reach your own verdict.

CHAPTER ONE

The Background of NCLB

On January 8, 2002, President George W. Bush signed the No Child Left Behind Act (NCLB) into law. Surrounded by smiling members of the Democratic and Republican leadership, the President declared, "As of this hour, America's schools will be on a new path of reform, and a new path of results."[1] His signature initiated sweeping changes to the 37-year-old Elementary and Secondary Education Act and thrust the nation's educators, schools, and school districts into a new world of federal educational leadership.

The President was not the new law's only cheerleader. The crowd of Democrats and Republicans around the President reflected the fact that, in the wake of the September 11, 2001, terrorist attacks on the World Trade Center and the Pentagon, NCLB had benefited from a wave of national unity and passed both houses of Congress with large, bipartisan majorities. The U.S. Senate supported the new law 87–10, and the House of Representatives endorsed it 381–41. Senate Republicans supported the law

44–3 and House Republicans voted for it 183–33. Democrats backed the law 43–6 in the Senate and 198–6 in the House.

Representative John Boehner, a Republican from Ohio and the chairman of the House Committee on Education and the Workforce, termed the law his "proudest achievement" in his years on Capitol Hill. Meanwhile, Ted Kennedy, a longtime Senator from Massachusetts and the ranking Democrat on the Senate Health, Education, Labor, and Pensions (HELP) Committee, proclaimed, "This is a defining issue about the future of our nation and about the future of democracy, the future of liberty, and the future of the United States in leading the free world. No piece of legislation will have a greater impact or influence on that."[2]

Early press coverage was positive. Friendly stories applauded Bush, Boehner, Kennedy, and other key Congressional leaders as they jetted around the country on a barnstorming tour that featured smiling schoolchildren and good-natured jokes about testing and homework.

By 2004, when President Bush stood for reelection, however, the era of easy good feelings had dissipated. During 2004, Democratic nominee John Kerry attacked NCLB as an empty promise, arguing, "Resources-without-reform is a waste of money, and reform-without-resources is a waste of time." Kerry accused the Bush administration of leaving "funding for NCLB $27 billion short of the promised levels, literally leaving millions of children behind."[3] Senator Kennedy accused the administration of reneging on its commitment to spend as much as promised on NCLB, and more than a dozen states expressed interest in throwing off the mandates embodied in the ambitious law. In Virginia, the Republican-controlled House of Delegates voted 98–1 to condemn NCLB for "represent[ing] the most sweeping intrusions into state and local control of education in the history of the United States."[4]

In early 2005, Nel Noddings, the president of the National Academy of Education and a faculty member at Columbia University's famed Teachers College, penned a very public attack on No Child Left Behind in the pages of *Education Week*. In an essay that summarized the complaints voiced by many critics, Noddings wrote, "My thesis is simple: The No Child Left Behind Act is a bad law, and a bad law is not made better by fully funding it." She explained, "The law employs a view of motivation that many of us in education find objectionable. As educators, we would not use threats, punishments, and pernicious comparisons to 'motivate' our students. But that is how the No Child Left Behind law treats the school establishment."

Noddings went on to observe, "The high-stakes testing associated with the law seems to be demoralizing teachers, students, and administrators. . . . . The law seems to be a corrupting influence. Again, we need more documentation. But reports suggest that cheating has increased at every level, and administrators are busily seeking loopholes, using triage techniques, moving kids around and reclassifying them, playing with data—all to meet the letter of a law whose actual requirements cannot reasonably be met. . . . If the No Child Left Behind Act is corrupting, we should get rid of it . . . We should not waste more valuable resources—human and monetary—tinkering with this law. It is a bad law and should be repealed."[5]

Criticism of NCLB came from the right as well as the left. In a 2005 policy report issued by the libertarian Cato Institute, former U.S. Department of Education staff member Lawrence Uzzell attacked NCLB for "virtually guarantee[ing] massive evasion of its own intent, ordering state education agencies to do things that they mostly don't want to do. Washington will be forced either to allow states great leeway in how they implement NCLB or to make NCLB more detailed, prescriptive, and top-heavy. If Washington chooses the former, the statute might as well not exist; if the latter, federal policymakers will increasingly resemble Soviet central planners trying to improve economic performance by micromanaging decisions from Moscow. NCLB may end up giving us the worst possible scenario: unconstitutional consolidation of power in Washington over the schools, with that power being used to promote mediocrity rather than excellence."[6]

Meanwhile, NCLB was vigorously defended by the Bush administration and a sometimes surprising array of allies. U.S. Secretary of Education Margaret Spellings, who replaced former Secretary Rod Paige at the beginning of the Bush administration's second term, declared in a speech in spring 2005, "In states where the law has been embraced, it is working. Teachers, principals, superintendents, parents and children have all chosen to roll up their sleeves and meet the challenge. As a result, children are achieving, and the achievement gap in the early grades is closing. In those states, public confidence in public education is soaring." In concluding, Spellings opined, "This law is a bipartisan expression of the fact that we as a nation no longer find it acceptable to let some children remain in the shadows, without the skills to achieve the American dream."[7]

Spellings's view drew sympathy from some unexpected quarters. In the summer of 2005, Robert Gordon, an education advisor to Democratic nominee Senator John Kerry during the 2004 general election, attacked Democratic criticism of NCLB as a betrayal of liberal values and as politically tone-deaf. Writing in *The New Republic*, a prominent center-left magazine, Gordon argued, "Progressives are misled by the logic of their own Bush-hatred: Bush is for NCLB, so NCLB must be bad. Never mind that President Clinton embraced accountability before President Bush. . . . At a time when Americans seek strength in their leaders, Democrats should find the strength to speak hard truths about our school and support essential changes." Gordon wrote, "The first task is to stop the unprincipled attacks on NCLB. At its heart, this is the sort of law liberals once dreamed about. . . . The law requires a form of affirmative action: States must show that minority and poor students are achieving proficiency like everyone else, or else provide remedies targeted to the schools those students attend."[8]

Striking a similar note, Ross Wiener, policy director of the liberal Education Trust, argued in summer 2005 that, "NCLB's accountability provisions are sparking progress. Many states, including Virginia, are narrowing previously stubborn gaps and boosting overall achievement. While the law certainly isn't perfect, these early results are too encouraging to allow the clock to be turned back on NCLB's accountability provisions." Wiener critiqued Republican Senator George Allen, a frequent Bush ally, for proposing changes that would turn back the clock on NCLB "and allow states simply to walk away from their responsibility to educate African American, Latino, and low-income students." Wiener closed on a bipartisan note, writing, "Fortunately, Congress has held firm in its support for greater educational equity. The Democrats and Republicans who worked together to give the nation a new tool for equity in public education have so far rebuffed every attempt to weaken the law."[9]

Why was NCLB hailed so enthusiastically at its passage; how did this popular law so quickly become a subject of fierce debate, and why do the battle lines sometimes slice across traditional boundaries? What is it that makes NCLB such an important law? How does NCLB actually work, and what does it mean for America's educators, parents, and children? These are the questions that this book will tackle. In this first chapter, we begin by discussing the origins of the No Child Left Behind Act.

The Legacy of the Elementary and Secondary Education Act (ESEA)

In the early 1960s, education proponents had spent more than a decade struggling to pass legislation that would provide federal support for K-12 schooling. Their efforts had met with little success, due to southern racial politics, church-state tensions in the north, and Republican resistance to expanding the role of the federal government. Southern

Democrats—and almost all elected officials from the "Solid South" were Democrats—opposed any federal law that would dictate to states or school districts how they should treat schools serving black students. In particular, in the years after the Supreme Court's 1954 *Brown v. Topeka Board of Education* desegregation decision, the Southern states were doing everything they could to resist integration and wanted no federal initiative to undercut that effort. Meanwhile, northern liberals insisted that any law treat black and white children equally.

A second impasse concerned the question of Catholic schools, many of them located in northern cities such as Boston, New York, and Chicago. Influential congressmen from these communities insisted that any federal aid for needy students should support children in both public and private schools. To do otherwise, they argued, would be unfair and an act of religious bigotry. Many of these voices were liberal Democrats representing Catholic constituencies. Meanwhile, other liberal Democrats who wanted to maintain a clear separation between church and state were opposed to any legislation that sent money to religious schools.

Finally, Republicans were concerned about efforts to expand the federal role in education. The U.S. Constitution makes no mention of education, and schooling has always been primarily left to state and local control. Republicans were concerned that increasing federal spending on K-12 schooling would eventually lead the federal government to play a more intrusive role in education policy and practice.

Given this deadlock, champions of federal education spending enjoyed little success through the Republican Eisenhower presidency of 1953–1961, except for the establishment of a few math and science programs created in the wake of the Soviet Union's launch of the *Sputnik* satellite. Even after Democrat John F. Kennedy won the presidency in 1961, while the Democrats enjoyed control of both houses of Congress, champions of federal education spending were stymied by the racial politics of the south and the religious politics of the north.

Kennedy's 1963 assassination, however, ushered in a new chapter in American politics. Following Kennedy's death, his Vice President Lyndon B. Johnson assumed the Presidency, strong-armed landmark civil rights legislation through Congress, and won the 1964 Presidential election in a landslide. Backed by massive Democratic majorities in the House and Senate, and having shown he could break the resistance of the southerners by passing the 1964 Civil Rights Act, Johnson forged a compromise education bill that won passage as the groundbreaking 1965 **Elementary and Secondary Education Act (ESEA).**

In 1964, when he announced his intention to enact social programs that would help construct a "**Great Society**," Johnson named three places where he intended to begin: in cities, in the countryside, and in the nation's classrooms. After discussing measures targeting urban and rural areas, he declared, "A third place to build the Great Society is in the classrooms of America. There your children's lives will be shaped. Our society will not be great until every young mind is set free to scan the farthest reaches of thought and imagination. We are still far from that goal. . . . Poverty must not be a bar to learning, and learning must offer an escape from poverty."[10]

The original ESEA included five titles. The heart of the law was a program of aid for the education of disadvantaged children. This provision, **Title I,** was supplemented by four other programs that addressed the purchase of instructional resources, the development of innovative curriculum or instructional techniques, grants to enhance the capabilities of state educational agencies, and support for educational research. The vast majority of ESEA spending was allocated to the law's first provision, Title I, which helped to pay for compensatory education programs. Title I funding was distributed through a formula that ensured at least some money went to almost every school district in the nation. In fact, the formula for allocating Title I aid resulted in 94% of all school

The Elementary and Secondary Education Act (ESEA)

first enacted in 1965, is the principal law affecting K-12 education

Great Society

a series of social programs originated by President Johnson that expanded the role of the federal government

Title I

the first and most important section of ESEA and refers to programs aimed at America's most disadvantaged students

districts receiving aid. Districts used Title I funding for a wide variety of initiatives, including parent training, speech therapy, medical services, socialization skills, and so on. Ted Sizer, former dean of the Harvard University Graduate School of Education, has observed, "ESEA was a political masterpiece, outside of its effect on education. Everybody had a finger in the pie."[11] In the two years following the adoption of ESEA, the U.S. Office of Education's annual budget nearly tripled, from $1.5 billion to $4 billion a year.

From the inception of ESEA, there were concerns that schools were inadequately educating disadvantaged students and were not being held accountable for their effectiveness. In securing the passage of the bill, the U.S. Commissioner of Education Francis Keppel had to address the concerns of Senator Robert F. Kennedy of New York, a Democrat and the younger brother of former President Kennedy, who worried that schools were doing a poor job educating black children. Keppel promised that the results of ESEA would be carefully evaluated, using objective measures to determine what children had learned. The reality, however, was that it would be years until such studies were launched. While the extensive "Sustaining Effects" study was pursued in the 1970s, and a careful evaluation was mounted after the 1988 **reauthorization**, it would be the 1990s before any real discussion would begin about holding schools and districts responsible for the academic achievement of Title I students.[12]

Reauthorization

the legislative process of renewing a program that is set to expire, sometimes with significant changes

Congress expanded ESEA's funding, regulations, and governmental reach through the late 1960s and the 1970s. Few were fully satisfied with the results of ESEA expansion, however. While ESEA succeeded at directing additional funds into schools serving disadvantaged children, the money was spread across so many schools and districts that its actual impact was limited. Meanwhile, economic stagnation and the exodus of the middle class from the inner cities fueled concerns about America's social stability and economic competitiveness. By the 1980s, there were concerns that America was lagging behind international competitors like Japan and the Soviet Union and that public schools were not effectively preparing the next generation for the challenges ahead.

A Nation at Risk

In 1981, Secretary of Education Terence Bell, named by newly elected Republican President Ronald Reagan, appointed a National Commission on Excellence in Education to examine American schooling. The commission issued its report, entitled *A Nation at Risk*. The aftermath reshaped the national education landscape. In bold, urgent language, the report charged that American schools were tolerating mediocrity. It urged states to adopt tougher standards, stronger graduation requirements, more rigorous curriculum, better pay for teachers, and improved teacher training.

A Nation at Risk triggered an outpouring of attention to education and spurred a series of influential state-level reform efforts. Governors in states like North Carolina, Texas, Tennessee, and Arkansas took the report's recommendations to heart and pushed for various reforms. Meanwhile, a raft of new studies, books, and task forces proposed a variety of measures, including calls to raise graduation standards, boost teacher pay, test teacher skills, and extend the school year. By 1984, the turmoil sparked by *A Nation at Risk* would cause the public, for the first time, to rank education as a significant issue in a presidential election. Nonetheless, even in the report's wake, the 1984 Republican platform argued against expanded federal educational efforts, declaring, "From 1965–1980 the U.S. indulged in a disastrous experiment with centralized direction of our schools."[13]

Education again ranked as a significant public concern during the 1988 election. A 1987 Gallup poll reported that 84% of Americans thought the federal government should require state and local educational authorities to meet minimum national standards. Republicans were opposed to such federal intrusion into local schools, however, which put them in an awkward position when faced with public demands for the government to do something. In fact, in 1988, by the margin of 55% to 22%, the public thought Democrats would do a better job of improving education than Republicans.[14]

In the course of his 1988 campaign for the presidency, Republican Vice President George H.W. Bush, a foreign policy specialist who had been director of the CIA and U.S. Ambassador to the United Nations, announced that he hoped to be known as the "Education President." Shortly after his victory, Bush convened the nation's governors in Charlottesville, Virginia, for their first-ever summit on education. At that historic 1989 meeting, Bush and the governors agreed on the importance of setting national goals. Working with the National Governors Association, the White House developed six national goals that Bush announced in his 1990 State of the Union address. The agenda aimed by the year 2000 for all children to start school "ready to learn"; a national high school graduation rate of at least 90%; student mastery of five core subjects before leaving grades four, eight, and twelve; American students to lead the world in math and science; all American adults to be literate and prepared for work and citizenship; and every school to be safe and drug-free. President Bush established a National Goals Panel, charged with tracking progress towards these goals, but the Panel struggled with a lack of reliable information on student performance and was buffeted by disagreement about how to reconcile state independence with national educational objectives.[15]

While *A Nation at Risk* gave birth to this focus on outcomes and standards, it also stirred a reform effort to increase parental choice and inject more competition into education. Choice-based reformers were concerned that schooling was overly bureaucratic and gave disadvantaged families little freedom to act as education consumers. Their reforms called for measures that would enable families to select their child's school and inject competition into the public schooling sector. Drawing on late-1960s proposals to offer "school vouchers" to poor children and to create "magnet schools," choice-based reforms in the 1980s generally amounted to little more than open enrollment programs in which states would permit students to cross school district lines. By 1990, however, proposals for school vouchers and charter schooling had made significant headway. The first school voucher program was introduced in Milwaukee, Wisconsin, in 1990 and permitted a limited number of low-income children to attend private schools with public support. **School vouchers** provide families with a specified amount of public funding with which to send a student to a public or private school of their choice.

The first charter law was enacted in Minnesota in 1991. **Charter schools** are public schools that are "chartered" by the state or by a state-authorized body and that operate independently of traditional school districts. Charter schools are funded on the basis of student enrollment and held accountable primarily on the basis of performance. In many ways, charter schools represent the intersection of standards-based reform with choice-based reform. Embraced by Republicans, centrist Democrats, and many urban reformers, charter schooling would grow rapidly. By the time No Child Left Behind was proposed in 2001, there existed more than 2,000 charter schools with an enrollment of over 500,000 students.

By the early 1990s, Republican and Democratic leaders largely agreed that the challenges identified by *A Nation at Risk* would not be solved simply through better texts and curricula, but would require a reshaping of the nation's schools. The Washington-driven remedies urged by Presidents George Bush and Bill Clinton both shared a commitment to higher standards, an increased focus on the measurement of student achievement, an embrace of more public school choice, and a faith in the importance of educational accountability. Where Bush had termed his package of education proposals "America 2000," Clinton termed his 1994 initiative "Goals 2000"—but few outside the federal bureaucracy could spot

School Vouchers provide families with a specified amount of public funding with which to send a student to a public or private school of their choice

Charter schools independent public schools of choice designed and operated by educators, parents, and other members of the community

major differences. Both started with the belief that U.S. schoolchildren were not learning enough, especially when it came to the "three Rs," and that the solution required inducing states to set explicit academic standards, deploy tests to determine whether and how well students and schools meet those standards, and create behaviorist "accountability" mechanisms that would assign rewards and provide for interventions or sanctions based on test outcomes. Well before NCLB, governors of both parties had embraced this strategy and a number of states had acted upon it, with varying degrees of enthusiasm.

The 1994 ESEA Reauthorization

Like all federal legislation, ESEA had to be "reauthorized" at regular intervals, typically every five or six years. Reauthorizations in the 1970s and 1980s expanded the law, added new provisions, and tinkered with formulas, but did not seek to revisit ESEA's fundamental design. The first effort at truly reshaping ESEA occurred during the reauthorization of 1994. President Bill Clinton sought to use the 1994 reauthorization to build on previous state efforts and on "America 2000." In so doing, he advanced a companion piece of legislation, entitled "Goals 2000," that required every state to create a standards-based education system that would apply to all students.

Under the new ESEA and "Goals 2000," states were required to establish academic standards in each grade and create tests to assess whether students had mastered the standards. The tests were to be administered to all poor children at least once in grades 3 through 5, 6 through 9, and 10 through 12. The ability of the federal Department of Education to enforce the provisions was quite limited, however, largely because of concerns at the White House that Republicans would attack a more intrusive approach as an example of "big government." In fact, during the 1994 Congressional elections, the Republicans enjoyed enormous success by touting their "Contract with America," which called for abolishing the U.S. Department of Education and rolling back the power of the federal government. Republicans claimed both the House and the Senate from the Democrats that year. Tom Payzant, Clinton's assistant secretary for elementary and secondary education at the time, has remarked, "The underlying policy direction of NCLB is consistent with the 1994 reauthorization, but there's a level of prescriptions with respect to **implementation** that [Democrats] would have been soundly criticized for trying to accomplish, had we done so."[16]

Implementation
putting government programs into effect

Despite the various compromises it had struck, the Clinton administration regarded the 1994 ESEA as a radical break with earlier versions of the law. The 1994 updates required, for the first time, that all states create performance-based accountability systems for schools by 2000. Facing a federal government that lacked any meaningful way to enforce the provisions, however, most states failed to comply. In 1999, Secretary of Education Richard Riley noted that just 36 states issued school report cards; only 19 provided assistance to low-performing schools, and just 16 had the authority to close down failing schools.[17] Moreover, many schools with Title I students were not even aware that the "major" 1994 shift in policy had taken place. As late as 2002, two years after the target date for full compliance, just 16 states had fully complied with the 1994 law. The 1994 reauthorization did succeed, however, in streamlining the regulations that had sprouted up around ESEA, with the Department of Education reporting that it had eliminated two-thirds of the rules previously associated with ESEA and had consolidated the required state applications into a much simpler form.

In 1999, ESEA was again due for reauthorization. That May, the Clinton administration forwarded a proposal that built on the 1994 law, with requirements that states regularly test all students—not just poor students—and language designed to heighten the pressure on states to comply with the law. A group of centrist Democrats, led by Senator Joe Lieberman, developed an alternative proposal to streamline federal funding and promote standards and accountability. This "New Democrat" proposal attracted much attention but did not go anywhere. Meanwhile, a group of Republicans on Capitol Hill, prodded by conservatives concerned about federal overreaching, opposed language to strengthen the ineffective accountability measures of the 1994 reauthorization. Conservative Republicans developed their own proposal, called the Academic Achievement for All Act ("Straight A's"), that sought to shift power and money back to the states by block-granting most federal education programs. With the 2000 election nearing, all of these proposals died a quiet death.

The Creation of NCLB

During the 2000 campaign, both presidential candidates promised aggressive action on education. Texas governor George W. Bush promoted as a national model his state's strong and relatively successful standards-based accountability program, leavened with charter schools and other elements of school choice. Vice President Al Gore sounded a remarkably similar note when he said: "Every state and every school district should be required to identify failing schools, and work to turn them around—with strict accountability for results, and strong incentives for success. And if these failing schools don't improve quickly, they should be shut down fairly and fast, and when needed, reopened under a new principal."[18] Gore also favored limited forms of school choice—as had President Bill Clinton.

In 2001, George W. Bush claimed the presidency after a campaign in which he expressly touted the results of Texas school reform. Seeking to vault the obstacles that had blocked earlier federal efforts to boost pupil achievement, he advocated a more forceful role for the national government—one that would use mandated tests and consequences to compel state and school cooperation, while increasing parental choice of schools and granting states more freedom in spending federal aid. Within days of taking office, Bush sent a legislative blueprint to Capitol Hill that drew heavily on his experience in Austin. The slender 26-page document, titled "No Child Left Behind," rested on four principles. It sought to "increase accountability for student performance," "focus on what works," "reduce bureaucracy and increase flexibility," and "empower parents."[19] The Bush proposal met with a favorable reaction from centrist "New Democrats," who noted that many elements of the White House proposal were similar to the ideas they had outlined for the 1999 reauthorization. One Democratic congressional aide who worked at the Department of Education under Clinton said, "The Bush administration took the Clinton administration's ideas and ran with them."[20] Whatever the truth of that particular claim, it is undeniable that the Bush administration's plan had important similarities to the 1999 Clinton proposal.

The White House proposal called for annual testing for all students in grades 3 through 8, with student performance publicly reported and broken out by race and class. Schools which failed to demonstrate acceptable performance for two straight years would be subjected to corrective action. If schools failed to perform adequately for three straight years, disadvantaged students would be permitted to use federal Title I funds to attend any high-performing public or private school of their choice—essentially transforming federal aid into a "voucher" redeemable at any effective school. States and schools were to be granted new flexibility under federal programs and regulations. For instance, the blueprint's proposals for teacher quality called for more flexibility in spending federal professional development dollars, measures to encourage states to embrace reforms like merit-based performance systems and bonus pay for teachers in high-need subject areas, and a fund to help develop systems to measure teacher performance based on student progress. The document also called for a federally funded "Reading First" initiative, improved math and science instruction, an emphasis on English fluency for "Limited English

Proficient" (LEP) students, efforts to promote innovative parental options and programs, and enhanced
school safety.[21]

In 2000, Democratic Senators Evan Bayh of
Indiana and Joseph Lieberman of Connecticut had
put forward a centrist ESEA reauthorization proposal
called the "Three Rs." Calling for more accountability in exchange for more state flexibility, some
of the proposal's recommendations were included in
the new White House legislation. Bayh, Lieberman,
and eight cosponsors reintroduced their bill the
same day Bush unveiled his new NCLB proposal
and were soon engaged in intense negotiations with
the White House. In February 2001, Senator Dianne
Feinstein, a Democrat from California, sent a letter
to President Bush indicating that she and many New
Democratic colleagues shared the White House's
emphasis on student results, its call for more local
flexibility, its support for parental choice and charter schooling, and its effort to cut back on federal regulation and bureaucracy.[22]

From the outset, however, the Bush administration sought broad-based bipartisan support that
stretched beyond centrist Democrats and included
more liberal members of Congress. Meanwhile, the
New Democrats themselves were leery of seeming too
out-of-step with the more liberal wing of the party.
For that reason, both Bush and the New Democrats
wanted NCLB to have the active backing of two
influential liberals—Massachusetts Senator Edward
M. Kennedy and California Representative George
Miller, the ranking Democratic members of Congress's
two education committees. To win their support,
the White House was willing to accept significant compromises. Significantly, early bargaining with Kennedy
and Miller led the White House to abandon its
voucher proposal and instead accept a proposal that
students in failing schools be allowed to use their Title
I money to pay for private tutoring. Negotiations
on how to determine whether a school was "failing" were long and complicated, and a spring 2001
Senate agreement unraveled because of concerns

that huge numbers of schools would be labeled failing under its performance goals.

Education policy debates were not the only challenges for the Bush administration as it worked to push ESEA reauthorization. In May of 2001, Senator Jim Jeffords, a liberal Republican from Vermont, declared himself an Independent and announced that he would caucus with the Democrats. Because the U.S. Senate had previously been perfectly split, 50–50, with Vice President Dick Cheney casting the decisive vote to give Republicans control of the body, Jeffords's action threw Senate control to the Democrats. Senator Kennedy became chairman of the Senate education committee; Jeffords took the reins of the environment committee and Republican Judd Gregg of New Hampshire became the ranking member of the education committee. Gregg joined Representative John Boehner of Ohio, Republican chair of the House Education and the Workforce Committee, and Kennedy and Miller to create the "Big Four" that would prove to be the key figures in molding NCLB.

In the end, the complex law that resulted from nearly a year's worth of negotiations featured ideas from left, right, and center—often without reconciling their inconsistencies. The final bipartisan measure commanded support not only from most Republicans but also from Kennedy, Miller, and the New Democrats. In many ways, NCLB's passage—just months after the terrorist attacks on the World Trade Center and the Pentagon—marked the high water mark of bipartisan comity after 9/11. One critical development was the way Bush's leadership silenced concerns about "big government" among conservatives who had helped to sink the Clinton administration's less ambitious 1999 proposal. Eager to support a conservative Republican president after eight years under a Democratic White House, conservatives who had championed the 1994 pledge to abolish the Department of Education swallowed their doubts and backed the Bush plan.

The price of broad congressional support was a radical overhaul of the original White House proposal.

The final, elephantine compromise bill joined Bush's quality-focused, results-centered approach to a host of equity-oriented provisions, while sharply curbing the White House's proposals for school choice and increased state flexibility. Though NCLB came to be seen as a "Bush" law—in no small part because the White House spent 2002 and 2003 claiming it as a major achievement, while Democrats spent much of 2003 and 2004 backing away from it—the reality is that the final bill's 681 finely printed pages were filled with a tangled assemblage of Bush administration proposals, New Democrat proposals drawn from reforms crafted during the Clinton administration, liberal ideas put forward by leading Democrats like Kennedy and Miller, and proposals and cautions introduced by countless other constituencies, all superimposed upon the ESEA template that had been growing and evolving since the 1960s.

The final bill proposed major departures on a few fronts and a host of smaller adjustments to ESEA. The most significant changes dealt with testing, accountability, and teacher quality. The testing and accountability provisions were championed by the Bush administration and its centrist Democratic allies and were largely consistent with the blueprint that the Bush administration initially proposed. The story was rather different when it came to teacher quality. As described in further detail in chapter 3, the Republicans on Capitol Hill made a strategic decision to turn the drafting of the law's **highly qualified teacher** provision over to Democrat George Miller, a veteran member with a long standing interest in teacher quality and a willingness to break with the teachers unions on the issue. Miller's handiwork yielded a set of prescriptive requirements, focused on ensuring that schools and students in poor communities were equipped to meet the law's challenges, that in many ways contrast with the results-in-return-for-flexibility approach embodied by the rest of NCLB. The final legislation also included a major federal initiative in the area of reading, an emphatic call for education policy and practice to be based

Highly qualified teachers

teachers who meet the standards established by the No Child Left Behind Act

> **Scientifically based research**
>
> is based on objective, empirical data collection and meets the criteria for scientific research

on **scientifically based research,** and a watered-down version of the flexibility proposals included in the President's original plan.

The final bill marked both a revolution in federal policy and a continued evolution of state and federal measures enacted in the 1980s and 1990s. One scholarly account suggested that NCLB was, on the one hand, the descendant of the various reforms that followed *A Nation at Risk,* but that, "In other respects, it has no precedent: it creates stern federal directives regarding test use and consequences; puts federal bureaucrats in charge of approving state standards and accountability plans; sets a single nationwide timetable for boosting achievement; and prescribes specific remedies for underperforming schools—and the children in them. In other words, NCLB marked both an evolutionary development and a revolutionary departure from existing policy."[23]

The NCLB "Theory of Action"

NCLB is a legislative compromise, assembled of many parts and composed of myriad ideas. Nonetheless, despite its sometimes fractured design, it is framed by a "theory of action" premised on the notion of holding schools and school districts accountable for student performance. It is useful to take a moment to clarify this theory of action before proceeding.

To begin, it is important to understand the problem that NCLB advocates intended to solve. First and foremost, they were concerned about the nation's "achievement gap"—primarily the disparity between the performance of white and Asian students, on the one hand, and African-American and Latino students, on the other. In 2000, the average African-American 12th grader was reading and performing math at approximately the same level as the average white 8th grader, a fact that leaders of both parties deemed morally unacceptable and a threat to American competitiveness in the global economy.[24] The willingness to accept sustained low levels of performance among black, Latino, and poor children was repeatedly attacked by Bush during his 2000 presidential campaign as "the soft bigotry of low expectations." NCLB assumes, in the words of Kati Haycock and Ross Wiener of the Education Trust, "That public education can teach, and has a responsibility to teach, almost every student how to read and do math up to a respectable level defined by the state. There is abundant evidence from schools all over the country that this is possible."[25]

Traditionally, there have been three competing explanations for the uneven performance of American students and the massive underperformance by black and Latino youths. One explanation faults a lack of resources, particularly money and know-how, in needy schools. A second traces the issue to problems in society and the larger culture, especially the effects of poverty. The third blames a dysfunctional school culture and a lax system of governance and incentives that permits school systems to avoid making unpopular decisions, even when those are essential to improving performance.

When it came to the funding issue, NCLB supporters were split, largely along party lines. In general, however, there was agreement that it made sense to provide increased resources in return for increased accountability. The question was how much money was enough. Republicans noted that the federal government had spent nearly $200 billion under ESEA since its 1965 adoption and yet had seemingly little to show for it. The White House called for more funding to support the specific testing and accountability components of NCLB and to fund the "Reading First" initiative but mostly argued that additional money was less important than changing the politics and culture of schooling. As we will see in chapter 4, much of the law's support from Democrats eventually softened over the issue of funding.

On the second and third explanations for the achievement gap—poverty and incentives—a broad agreement among Democrats and Republicans had taken root during the 1990s. Both Democrats and

Republicans vehemently rejected the notion that poverty, culture, or family were legitimate explanations for mediocre student performance. Its defenders explained the law's charge to schools in a simple phrase: "No excuses." While some supporters of the law, especially liberal Democrats, were also working to strengthen the nation's social safety net and fund other anti-poverty programs, they pointed to successful public schools in tough urban and rural environments as proof that difficult challenges could be overcome by excellent schools.

NCLB was predominantly intended to address the third explanation for the achievement gap: the systemic and political challenges of the nation's schools. The law is premised on the notion that local education politics are fundamentally broken, and that only strong, external pressure on school systems, focused on student achievement, will produce a political dynamic that leads to school improvement. Having lived with the disappointing results of the accountability provisions in the 1994 reauthorization of ESEA and frustrated by the tepid results wrought by decades of school reform, policymakers decided that high standards, meaningful sanctions, and federal leadership were essential if they were to change business as usual in the schools. They believed that school boards and superintendents would continue to be reluctant to upend dysfunctional routines or upset important constituencies, like teachers unions or affluent parents, unless pressed to do so. Ultimately, NCLB was intended to provide political cover to superintendents and school board members to encourage them to take controversial and difficult steps to root out mediocre teachers and administrators, shift resources to poorer schools, challenge collective bargaining provisions regulating teacher transfer and inhibiting efforts to link pay to teacher quality, and overhaul central office processes.

Critiquing NCLB's Theory of Action

Some critics questioned NCLB's focus on testing and accountability from the outset. Anti-testing crusader Alfie Kohn argued in January 2001, just days after the initial White House plan was unveiled, "The people who understand how kids learn are appalled at this. This is horrendous, simplistic, test-driven reform."[26] In a more scholarly but equally devastating appraisal, Harvard University education professor Richard F. Elmore declared, "Never, I think, in the history of federal education policy has the disconnect between policy and practice been so evident, and possibly never so dangerous. What's particularly strange and ironic is that conservative Republicans control the White House and the House of Representatives, and they sponsored the single largest—and the single most damaging—expansion of federal power over the nation's education system in history."[27] Beyond the simple opposition to standardized testing that Kohn vocalized, critics of the NCLB "theory of action" have tended to focus on four primary concerns.

First, they have worried that NCLB focuses on the achievement of a school's students at one moment in time rather than on progress over the course of the academic year, measuring school performance in a crude fashion that does not accurately reflect school quality. They have also argued that the law's guidelines for determining whether schools are making "adequate" progress are overly crude and that annual assessments are not reliable enough to accurately measure school performance. Thus, they argue, the accountability provisions are unlikely to channel political pressure in constructive ways.[28]

Second, critics have challenged the quality of state standards and tests, arguing that judging schools with poor tests will distort teaching while failing to accurately measure the most important knowledge and skills. In particular, they ask whether content mastery is well defined, whether tests measure the full range of relevant skills, whether test preparation is intruding on more worthwhile learning, and whether the focus on reading and math is squeezing history, science, and the arts out of the curriculum.[29]

Third, critics have argued that the law's expectation that all students will be 100% proficient in reading and math by 2014 is unrealistic and sets up schools and school districts for inevitable failure. In particular, critics have asserted that a child's social circumstances, home environment, and health care will have at least as great an impact on student achievement as classroom teaching. Therefore, they suggest that it is unfair to hold teachers and schools solely accountable for student performance.[30] Some critics have speculated that the law was designed to ensure most schools would eventually be deemed low-performing in an effort to undermine public schooling and promote measures such as school vouchers and the private management of schools.[31]

Finally, critics have raised questions about whether NCLB devotes sufficient attention to what actually makes schools successful. Harvard's Professor Elmore, for instance, has suggested that the emphasis on accountability reflects "a naïve" and "oversimplified" understanding of school improvement. He has argued, "School personnel must share a coherent, explicit set of norms and expectations about what a good school looks like before they can use signals from the outside to improve student learning. . . . Low-performing schools aren't coherent enough to respond to external demands for accountability."[32] In fact, such critics are concerned that NCLB's demands may make it more difficult for low-performing schools to attract quality staff or focus on improving student achievement.

How accurately NCLB actually diagnoses the obstacles to school improvement and how effectively it addresses these are questions that each reader must decide. With that aim in mind, let us now turn to the law itself.

GLOSSARY

Charter schools—are independent public schools of choice that are designed and operated by educators, parents, community leaders, educational entrepreneurs, and others. They are sponsored by designated public entities, such as local or state educational organizations that monitor their quality and effectiveness but allow them to operate outside the traditional system of public schools.

Elementary and Secondary Education Act (ESEA)—was first enacted in 1965 and is the principal federal law affecting K-12 education. The No Child Left Behind Act of 2001 is the most recent reauthorization of the ESEA.

Great Society—was a series of social programs legislated at the request of President Lyndon B. Johnson. It was a dramatic expansion of the federal government's role in state and domestic affairs.

Highly qualified teacher—is defined by NCLB as a teacher who has obtained full state teacher certification or has passed the state teacher licensing examination and holds a license to teach in the state; holds a minimum of a bachelor's degree; and has demonstrated subject area competence in each academic subject he or she teaches.

Implementation—occurs when the states, school districts, or other entities put into effect the procedures of any government program, including the No Child Left Behind Act.

Reauthorization—is the legislative process of renewing a program that is set to expire, sometimes with significant changes.

School vouchers—provide families with a specified amount of public funding with which to send a student to a public or private school of their choice.

Scientifically based research—is based on objective empirical data, employs appropriate modern methods of data collection and analysis, allows for repetition or expansion, and has been subject to peer review. The most desirable form of scientifically based research according to NCLB is the randomized-controlled study.

Title I—was the first and most important section of ESEA. It refers to programs aimed at America's most disadvantaged students. Title I, Part A offers assistance to improve the teaching and learning of children in high-poverty schools and to enable those children to meet challenging state academic content and performance standards.

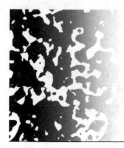

CHAPTER TWO

NCLB Testing, Accountability, and Choice

The No Child Left Behind Act sought to shift federal education policy from its historic emphasis on redistributing money and regulating how that money was spent to a focus on the performance of students, schools, and school districts. This shift required the federal government to develop guidelines for setting academic expectations, measuring academic outcomes, and prescribing remedies for schools and districts that fail to meet performance expectations. As we discussed in Chapter 1, this marked a radical change in federal policy. Until the 1990s, it was presumed that the proper federal role was helping to alleviate inequities that resulted from an uneven distribution of "inputs" (such as money, materials, facilities, and good teachers) across communities. Federal oversight was restricted to ensuring that assistance was spent for its intended purposes, while questions of performance, student achievement, and school improvement were deemed the province of the states.

In truth, almost from the enactment of ESEA in 1965, the introduction of federal funding meant that the federal government started to make decisions that affected schools and school districts. Federal funds inevitably brought rules and regulations in their wake. Lawmakers were concerned, for example, that federal education funds be spent on activities and children for which they were intended. At one time, schools even went to the point of labeling particular school supplies, e.g., staplers, as belonging to "Title I," the main federal program. If a non-Title I teacher dared to use the Title I stapler, the school could be deemed "out of compliance" with federal guidelines.

After decades of efforts to improve schools by redistributing funds and micromanaging procedures, reformers expressed growing frustration with the lack of evident results. They worried that the proliferation of rules, programs, and regulations was actually making it more difficult for educators to make sensible decisions. By the 1990s, there was widespread agreement that there should be less attention to "inputs" and more to "outcomes" such as student achievement and graduation rates. Meanwhile, in the years after *A Nation at Risk,* states began to set standards for what students in a given grade should know and be able to do. The hope was that teachers would align their lesson plans with these standards and that students, teachers, and administrators would strive to meet them.

It soon became clear that setting standards was only a starting point. Raising student achievement would also require states to measure whether students were in fact reaching the standards and to link consequences to success and failure. In other words, improving the system required policymakers to get the incentives right for educators and for students. In the late 1980s and early 1990s, leading states such as Texas, Virginia, North Carolina, and Massachusetts built whole accountability systems around their academic standards—setting requirements for what students needed to know, measuring to see that students knew it, and judging schools based on how their students were performing.

In the course of the 2000 presidential election, in which Texas Governor George W. Bush was a central figure, scholars and policy experts paid particular attention to the experiences of two southern states—North Carolina and Texas. Both states had posted impressive gains through the 1990s on the **National Assessment of Educational Progress**—the test known as "the nation's report card." Minority students, especially, were making huge strides in the two states, both of which had built their reform efforts around robust accountability systems.[1]

National Assessment of Educational Progress
the only nationally representative and continuing assessment of American students' achievements

NCLB represented an effort to extend Texas-flavored, test-based accountability to the entire country. While the law forced some states to create an accountability apparatus more or less from scratch, for the majority of states NCLB required the addition of new features to systems already in place. The signature innovation of NCLB, based largely on the Lone Star State system, was the requirement that states hold schools accountable not just for the overall performance of their students but also for the performance of individual **subgroups**: ethnic and racial groups, low-income students, students with disabilities, and students with limited English proficiency. This feature was central to the law's rhetoric: Because "no child" would be hidden by a school's average test scores, the law would ensure that "no child" would be left behind.

Subgroup
a group of students within a school population with a group-specific background or characteristics

The NCLB accountability system rests on the requirement that states develop challenging content standards for what students are expected to know and be able to do, create state assessments that mirror these content standards, and annually test students to measure competency in the "core subjects" of reading and math. To help states and schools do the required work and meet the new expectations, NCLB's framers called for increased Title I funding for schools serving disadvantaged students and required school districts to provide extra assistance for struggling schools. Ultimately, NCLB calls for all states to reach **universal proficiency** in reading and math by 2013–2014. By that date, states are

Universal proficiency
the final goal of NCLB for all students to achieve proficiency in math, English, and the other core academic subjects

to ensure that all students, including those in the lowest achieving schools and districts, are able to meet state content standards. What "universal proficiency" means and what state content standards entail are important, somewhat ambiguous considerations that we will discuss shortly.

Importantly, while NCLB puts great pressure on schools and school districts to improve student learning, the law does not include incentives or consequences for students themselves. Schools are not required to tie student promotion policies to test results, nor are they required to withhold high school diplomas from students who fail the state tests. Several states have adopted such policies on their own initiative, but under the federal law, it is schools and districts that are to be held accountable, not students.

On paper, at least, the accountability system sounds reasonably straightforward. As President Bush pointed out shortly before the beginning of his second term, "If you believe every child can learn, then it makes sense to measure to determine whether every child is learning. That's called accountability, accountability for results. Accountability is so crucial to achieve our goal for every child learning to read, write, add and subtract."[2]

In practice, the arrangements are quite complicated and look remarkably different from state to state. The measurement system envisioned in NCLB requires that states develop three related components: standards, assessments, and accountability. Standards are the material that students are expected to know; assessments are the tests used to measure whether they have learned the material in the standards, and accountability is the system of remedies and rewards that recognizes high performance and addresses poor performance by schools and school districts.

Standards and Assessments

Like all federal efforts to improve public education, NCLB sketches out broad requirements and then leaves key details to the judgment of Department of Education officials and to the individual states. With regard to standards, though not with accountability, NCLB gives little concrete guidance to states. NCLB requires that state plans "demonstrate that the State has adopted challenging academic content standards and challenging student academic achievement standards," but also makes clear that these standards need not be approved by the U.S. Department of Education. In other words, the law requires states to develop standards, but it says nothing about the actual content or rigor of the standards themselves. For example, should multiplication of simple digits be taught in second grade or third? Should students be required to know the year the Civil War began or how many justices sit on the Supreme Court? Such decisions, and all other curricular determinations, are left to the individual states. NCLB does not offer guidance on what should be included in the standards, what state tests should assess, or how state tests ought to be scored. The law simply requires states to devise their own standards and create tests that reflect those standards. The law does call for a "peer review" process to ensure the technical soundness of state testing systems, but even this requirement is focused on the process rather than the substance of testing.

NCLB mandates that state academic *content* standards specify what children are expected to know and what they should be able to do at each grade level. It also requires states to set academic *achievement* standards, which must define three **levels of achievement**: basic, proficient, and advanced. For each assessment, the state must determine the score students have to achieve to reach each of these levels. NCLB's charge is that states ensure that, by 2014, all students will be performing at or above the proficient level. Again, determining the definition of basic, proficient, and advanced is left up to each state.

In order to determine whether or not their students are meeting academic standards, states must develop reading and math tests that measure student learning. NCLB requires that tests in reading and math be administered every year in grades 3–8 and

Levels of achievement
levels of students' proficiency in math, English, and science, and the other core academic subjects

at least once in high school. States are also required to design and administer an annual science assessment by the 2007–2008 school year and must test students at least once in grades 3 through 5, 6 through 9, and 10 through 12. The reading, math, and science assessments must "cover the breadth and depth of state content standards," be "reliable and of high technical quality," and report student results in terms of the required state achievement standards (e.g., basic, proficient, or advanced).

States can use either "criterion-referenced" or "-norm-referenced" tests and are permitted to utilize a mixture of statewide and local assessments. ("Criterion-referenced" tests judge student performance relative to particular expectations for student learning, whereas "norm-referenced" tests measure students' proficiency against the performance of their peers.)

In rare cases, NCLB assessments are developed at the local level, typically by a district or a set of districts. If local assessments are used, they must be readily aggregated into the larger pool of data that states collect from all schools and districts for analysis and comparison. Such assessments are also required to be equal in rigor and reliability to the state assessment or to other local assessments. Only one state—Nebraska—has attempted to use local assessments in its NCLB accountability system.

NCLB also requires that states make accommodations for students with disabilities and that includes native-language versions of assessments for students with limited English proficiency, though students who have attended school in the United States for three years or more must be tested in English. In addition to the academic content assessments, states must develop English proficiency exams that assess the oral language and reading and writing skills of students with limited English proficiency. These exams must be administered annually to assess student progress toward English proficiency.

To make the performance of public schools and districts more transparent, NCLB requires districts to publish and disseminate student achievement results in a timely and accessible fashion. The law's authors hoped that public outcry over lackluster scores will force schools to raise their sights and focus on students who have been left behind. NCLB clearly defines the district's responsibility to make public the results of annual testing. The disaggregated results must be made publicly available before the beginning of the next school year, and districts must "publicize and disseminate the results of the annual review . . . to parents, teachers, principals, schools, and the community so that the teachers, principals, other staff, and schools can continually refine, in an instructionally useful manner, the program of instruction." Based on the initial results, districts are to evaluate each school's professional development and efforts to promote parental involvement. In practice, many states and districts have failed to provide all of the required information by the stipulated deadline.

Standards and assessments in and of themselves can shed light on educational performance but do not necessarily have consequences or lead to change. Making accountability consequential requires policymakers to link sanctions or rewards to results. This requires policymakers to first answer a few basic questions. How much student achievement is enough? Is the goal for students to reach a set bar or to make progress over time? Should attention be focused on the average performance of a school's students or the performance of individual subgroups, like African-American or poor children? No Child Left Behind's answer to these questions is a formula known as "adequate yearly progress."

Adequate Yearly Progres

Adequate yearly progress (AYP) is the measure by which all schools and school districts are evaluated under NCLB. The law's fundamental dictate is that all schools and districts "make AYP." The concept of "making AYP" can be compared to schools and districts jumping over a bar. The bar is the percentage of children that must score "proficient" on

Adequate yearly progress (AYP)
the minimum level of improvement schools and school districts need to make every year under NCLB

the math and reading assessments. Over time, states must raise the bar so that, by 2013–2014, it is set at 100%, or universal proficiency. A state could deem a school to be making AYP if 40% of its students were "proficient" in reading in 2005, and 70% in 2009, so long as the state ramped up expectations so that they reached 100% by 2013–2014. Because states have considerable leeway to decide how aggressively to raise the AYP bar over time, some critics have noted that NCLB may invite gaming of the system by states that wish to minimize the number of schools that fail to make AYP. For instance, a number of states, such as Alaska, Ohio, and Arizona, have "back-loaded" their accountability systems so that the percentage of students who need to achieve proficiency moves up rather slowly until about 2010 and then skyrockets to 100% by 2013–2014. Some scholars have termed this the "balloon mortgage" approach to setting performance goals because it makes short-term goals more attainable only by accepting a steep long-term obligation.

One can imagine, then, that a state with a tough definition of proficiency and a high bar for AYP would identify many more schools as failing to make AYP than a state with a weak definition of proficiency and a low bar for AYP. In fact, by 2005, some states had virtually no schools identified as needing improvement while other states identified more than 70% of theirs as failing to clear the bar. A corollary is that "universal proficiency" will have very different meanings in different states. In some places with low standards, it will have little meaning at all.

Once states have administered their assessments and collected scores for every student, the law specifies how they are to analyze the data and calculate which schools and districts made AYP. NCLB requires that AYP determinations be "statistically reliable and valid"; be based primarily on state academic assessments, and include another indicator—graduation rates for high schools and, typically, attendance rates for elementary and middle schools. Because NCLB is focused primarily on academic achievement, gains on this second indicator cannot prevent a school or district from missing AYP. However, a drop in the graduation or attendance rate can result in a school failing to make AYP even if its achievement levels are satisfactory.

NCLB's Subgroups

Calculating AYP is not as simple as measuring the percentage of students in a school that meets or exceeds the proficiency standard. Instead, NCLB requires that states hold schools accountable for the achievement of each of the school's subgroups as well. This process of **disaggregation** involves calculating and reporting the performance for various subgroups of students. The mandate that states disaggregate their performance data is at the heart of No Child Left Behind accountability. Prior to NCLB, those states that had accountability systems generally held schools accountable for overall student performance or for the progress of students over time. While these systems were major innovations in their day, scholars and advocates expressed concern that they did not provide incentives to schools or districts to focus on the neediest children. Instead, schools could meet state expectations, even if whole groups of students—such as children living below the poverty line—were failing to achieve state standards. Such considerations led lawmakers to adopt the "Texas model" of subgroup disaggregation in NCLB and to take it to another level.

> **Disaggregation**
>
> means to separate a whole into its parts

Each state is required to analyze the achievement of the following subgroups of students within each school: all racial/ethnic groups present in the school (white, African-American, Latino, Native American, and so on); low-income students; students with disabilities; and students with limited English proficiency. In order for the school to make AYP, each of these subgroups must clear the AYP bar in reading and in math. (States must also calculate and report the proficiency rates of male and female students as well as migrant students, though these subgroups are not included in the AYP determination.) The data points used to judge a school, therefore, may include "Latino scores in math," "reading scores of low-income students," "special education student scores in math," and so on.

NCLB recognizes that at some schools these subgroups will be quite small or nonexistent. In order to protect student confidentiality and ensure some degree of statistical reliability, states are allowed to set the minimum size, also known as "n size," under which subgroup scores will not count. For instance, if a school has only two Native American students, the law's authors thought it capricious for the school to miss AYP because one of them failed the state exam. The state-adopted "n sizes" range from a low of five to a high of 100, with most clustering around 30 or 40. These differences are significant. Imagine two 800-student middle schools with exactly the same demographics but in different states—one with an "n" size of 30, the other with an "n" size of 90. Each school is 90% white and 10% African-American. In the state with an "n size" of 30, the subgroup scores of the school's 80 African-Americans would count. If only a small percentage of these students reached the proficient level on the state exams, the school would not make AYP. In the other state, with a minimum size of 90, the subgroup's scores would not count, and as long as the school's overall scores were high enough, it would make AYP.

In addition, the law sets a participation threshold for each group. The drafters of the law were concerned that some schools might encourage low-performing students to stay home the day of the test, in order to inflate results. Therefore, the law decreed that 95% of each group of students had to participate in the state exam each year in order for that school or district to be eligible to make AYP. For instance, even if a school's African-American population easily exceeded the AYP bar on the state assessment, if only 93% of the total number of African-American students took the exam, then the school would fail to make AYP.

Shortly after the enactment of NCLB, the participation provision was criticized as unrealistic. For instance, in Georgia, 187 schools failed to make AYP in 2002–2003 because they did not muster adequate student participation. In March 2004, the Department of Education responded to these concerns by announcing that schools would have additional flexibility in determining their participation rates. The revisions allow schools to average participation rates over three years in order to reach 95% and to excuse students from participating due to a medical emergency. For example, if 93% of a school's Latino population took the state test one year, the school could still make AYP if, in the two preceding years, 95% and 97% of Latino students took the exam. This flexibility is especially salient in states, such as California, that allow parents to opt their children out of state exams.

Safe Harbor

As No Child Left Behind wound its way through Congress, some advocates and educators expressed concern that the AYP formula would punish schools that started out with very low levels of student performance but that made great progress over time. They worried that, however rapidly these schools were raising achievement, the schools would still be unlikely to help enough students reach proficiency and make AYP. To satisfy these critics, Congress included the **safe harbor provision** in the law's final version. Under this provision, even a school that fails to clear the statewide bar in a given year can make AYP if it reduces the percentage of students who are not proficient by at least 10% from the previous year. This rule applies to the school's overall results as well as those of its subgroups.

Safe harbor
a provision intended to prevent the over-identification of schools not making AYP

For example, imagine a high school that meets almost all of its targets: reading achievement for all groups, participation rates, and graduation rates. It meets all of its math targets except for one: Only 37% of its Latino students are proficient in math; the target was 50%. However, the school could still make AYP under "safe harbor." How would this work? The previous year, only 30% of Latino students were proficient in math. Put another way, 70% were *not* proficient. Under Safe Harbor, the school had to decrease the percentage of Latino students who were not proficient by at least 10%. This required that the 70% be reduced by at least one-tenth, or by 7%. In other words, the school would make AYP provided the percentage of Latino students proficient in math was equal to at least 30% + 7%. Thus, rather than needing to reach 50% proficiency in math among the Latino subgroup, the school would make AYP by reaching 37%. The following year, of course, the "safe harbor" figure would rise to reflect the school's higher level of achievement. The logic of the 10% figure was that consistent gains of that size would ensure that even "safe harbor" schools were at 100% proficiency by 2013–14. Needless to say, the "safe harbor" provision is not well understood by educators or the public.

Students with Disabilities and Students with Limited English Proficiency

Some critics have been particularly skeptical about the testing requirements placed on students with disabilities and with limited English proficiency (LEP). These students had generally been exempt from state accountability systems, including Texas's. After all, many argued, if these students were achieving state standards, most would not be labeled as having disabilities or limited English proficiency. In response to such concerns, the Department of Education has, over time, modified the testing requirements for these students. In December 2003, Secretary of Education Rod Paige announced that schools would be allowed to exempt up to 1% of all students, or 10% of their special education students, from the regular testing regime. This policy was targeted at students with severe cognitive disabilities such as profound mental retardation. While the law's aim was to raise expectations for all students, everyone agreed that a small percentage of students would never be able to meet the regular standards. Even these

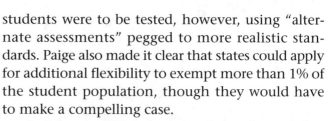

students were to be tested, however, using "alternate assessments" pegged to more realistic standards. Paige also made it clear that states could apply for additional flexibility to exempt more than 1% of the student population, though they would have to make a compelling case.

In February 2004, Secretary Paige decreed that schools would also have more flexibility in testing LEP students. Under the change, schools would not have to test students who are brand-new to the country (defined as having been here for less than one year) in reading, though they still had to test the students' skills in mathematics, using an exam in their native language, and their English language proficiency. Paige also issued a new policy attempting to address one of the law's most challenging features: as originally implemented, LEP students had to take reading and math tests in their own language, or, if translated tests were not available, they had to take the tests in English. However, if these students took a reading test in English and passed it, they would, by definition, no longer be considered LEP, and their scores would not count for the LEP subgroup. By this reasoning, only students who could not pass the test would remain in the LEP subgroup, and hence this subgroup would never be able to clear the proficiency bar. To address this conundrum, Paige allowed states to count students who had graduated from the LEP designation as members of the LEP group for up to two years.

In the spring of 2005, the new education secretary, Margaret Spellings, announced additional flexibility regarding the testing of students with disabilities. Schools would henceforth be allowed to exempt an additional 2% of students (those with learning disabilities) from taking the regular state assessment, above and beyond the 1% with the most severe cognitive disabilities. Instead, these learning-disabled students are allowed to take tests specifically geared toward their abilities. Some special education advocates worried that this new policy would lower standards for students with disabilities, whereas some educators and administrators voiced concern that the changes did not go far enough.

The process of disaggregating and evaluating school results by subgroup includes other wrinkles. One is that many students fall into more than one group, meaning that their failure to reach proficiency will adversely affect the prospect of each subgroup making AYP. For instance, an LEP Latino child from a disadvantaged family would fit into three different subgroups. If she failed to reach proficiency in reading or math, her performance would affect the reported performance of all three subgroups and her school's prospects of making AYP on each count.[3] While some educators regard this "multiple-counting" as unfair, NCLB proponents consider it a plus. They argue that certain groups of children—particularly minorities and those with special needs—have long been overlooked and that this kind of disaggregation helps ensure no one is ignored.

Concerns About the Testing Requirements

Various observers have raised concerns about NCLB's testing regime. Given the law's emphasis on standardized test results, it is not surprising that critics of testing have pilloried the law as harmful for students, teachers, and schools. Such critics tend to argue that testing narrows the curriculum, distracts teachers from focusing on student needs, and turns schools into factories that strive to pack information into inert students.[4] As high school principal and author George Wood has argued, "By limiting all school success measures to one test score, *the quality of schools will actually decline.*"[5] Such critics believe that excessive reliance on testing will force schools to cut out instruction in the arts and humanities. Stanford University education professor Linda Darling-Hammond believes that NCLB-style accountability does little to actually help improve schools. "The biggest problem with NCLB," she asserts, "is that it mistakes measuring schools for fixing them."[6] Such critics do not believe that NCLB's testing requirements need to be adjusted or refined but that the premise of the law is fundamentally misguided.

There are also skeptics who question NCLB's method of measurement. As it is currently designed, AYP is calculated using the absolute level of student performance at a given time. This approach gives schools and districts an idea of how close a particular group of students is to achieving universal proficiency, but it does not measure the rate at which individual students are improving from year to year. In other words, NCLB's current testing regime does not account for the **value-added** by schools. Some observers have advocated coupling the current AYP metric with a value-added system.[7] Such a combination would gauge the percentage of students reaching proficiency, while recognizing schools that do an excellent job of improving the achievement of the lowest-performing students from year to year, even if they do not make it to the "proficiency" bar. This method differs from NCLB's "safe harbor" provision in that it focuses on consistent gains rather than a particular portion of students reaching proficiency in a given year.

Concerns about NCLB's lack of a value-added measurement are especially acute for charter schools, which are generally new schools that enroll a disproportionate number of disadvantaged children. While a charter school's student population may not be achieving the absolute level of proficiency demanded by the state—largely because of the failures of its students' previous schools—it may nonetheless be producing significant achievement gains from year to year. Without a value-added metric, such a school would be deemed **in need of improvement** under NCLB's current system. For similar reasons, some middle school and high school advocates have complained that these institutions get blamed for the shortcomings of their feeder elementary schools.

In response to such concerns, Secretary Spellings announced in November 2005 that up to 10 states would be allowed to develop accountability systems that consider the progress of students over time. Spellings made it clear that to qualify for the addi-

Value-added measures a student's performance throughout the school year

In need of improvement schools in need of improvement receive Title I funds yet fail to make adequate yearly progress for two straight years

tional flexibility, a state's system must maintain high expectations for low-performing students and ensure that all groups of students are making enough progress to reach universal proficiency by 2013–2014.[8]

Sanctions for Failing to Make AYP

The standards and testing provisions themselves constitute only the first two-thirds of the NCLB accountability system. In order to actually hold schools accountable, testing results must be linked to consequences. Under NCLB, schools that fail to make AYP are subject to a series of cascading remedies, sanctions, and interventions intended both to compel schools to improve and afford additional options to students in low-performing schools. These interventions become increasingly intense if the school or district continues to fail for consecutive years, eventually resulting in major changes in school status, governance, staffing, or all of the above.

If a school fails to make AYP two years in a row, it is labeled "in need of improvement." Once in "improvement" status, district and school officials must explain to parents what the label signifies, how the school compares to other district schools, and what the school is doing to improve its rating. They

School improvement plan

a written document for Title I schools in need of improvement that outlines how to make the improvements

must also come up with a **school improvement plan** that covers a two-year period, is based on scientifically based research, focuses on core subjects, mandates increased professional development, and stimulates greater parental involvement. This improvement plan must pass peer review by the district and be implemented no later than the beginning of the next school year. Districts are obligated to provide technical assistance to help improvement schools implement their plan. While the requirements of school improvement plans seem rigorous on paper, the practical significance of these plans varies tremendously.

In addition to these school improvement activities, schools that fail to make AYP for two consecutive years must offer students the option of transferring to a public school within the district that is not "in need of improvement." Schools that fail to improve for a third straight year must provide

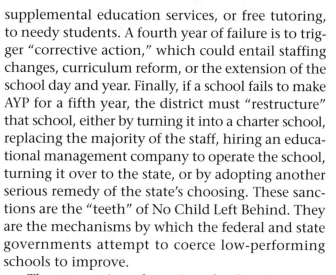

supplemental education services, or free tutoring, to needy students. A fourth year of failure is to trigger "corrective action," which could entail staffing changes, curriculum reform, or the extension of the school day and year. Finally, if a school fails to make AYP for a fifth year, the district must "restructure" that school, either by turning it into a charter school, replacing the majority of the staff, hiring an educational management company to operate the school, turning it over to the state, or by adopting another serious remedy of the state's choosing. These sanctions are the "teeth" of No Child Left Behind. They are the mechanisms by which the federal and state governments attempt to coerce low-performing schools to improve.

The progression of sanctions for districts is similar in intent but different in the particulars. NCLB basically treats districts as if they were one big school and then applies the same testing and AYP requirements. Each subgroup in the district must achieve AYP in a given subject for the district to make AYP. It is not unusual for districts to fail to make AYP, even if all of their schools do, given the minimum subgroup size rule. Low-performing subgroups might be too small to count at individual schools, but aggregating all the students at the district level can yield a group sufficiently large to derail a district's AYP designation. Districts that fail to make AYP for multiple years become subject to harsh "corrective actions" and eventually to complete restructuring, which could include a state takeover.

Applying AYP

NCLB's accountability requirements, including those governing assessment and the calculation of AYP, apply to all public schools. This means they apply to charter schools as well as traditional district schools. When it comes to NCLB's consequences, however, the sanctions and remedies that result from failing to make AYP only apply to schools that receive funding from NCLB's Title I program, also known as Title I schools. The Student Achievement and School Accountability office at the U.S.

Department of Education offers the following guidance on this policy:

> Under NCLB, a State must implement a single, statewide accountability system and make an annual determination of whether each public school, both schools that do and do not receive Title I funds, has made AYP. However, NCLB does not apply the requirements of section 1116 (regarding school improvement, corrective action, and restructuring) to schools that do not receive Title I funds.[9]

In other words, all schools must test at least 95% of their students, must disaggregate test data by subgroups, and must produce an AYP calculation, but only schools that receive Title I dollars are subject to NCLB's consequences. Of course, it is important to keep in mind that close to 60% of all America's public schools are Title I schools. Moreover, there are a few states that have chosen to apply these consequences to all public schools that fail to make AYP, and not only to Title I schools.

Charter schools, especially the vast majority that receive Title I dollars, are subject to the same testing and AYP requirements as all public schools. Because many charters do not register achievement gains in their first few years of operation, however, these schools benefit from the Department of Education's decision that new schools are not subject to AYP calculations until two years of achievement data are available. Due to their small size, many charters also benefit from the minimum subgroup size requirements discussed previously. Because of their small size, many charter schools will not have enough students for more than a handful of subgroups to be counted.

Public School Choice

Public school choice
Title I schools that do not make adequate yearly progress must offer all students the opportunity to transfer to another public school

The first of NCLB's cascading remedies is **public school choice**. Public choice enables students at Title I schools in need of improvement to transfer to another school within the district (one that is not "in need of improvement") or to a nearby charter school. What was the intent of this policy? First, many members of Congress thought it unfair to tell parents that their child's school was failing without providing them an opportunity to move elsewhere. Second, as with many reforms involving school choice, legislators hoped that parents would "vote with their feet" and move children to higher performing schools, pressuring poorly performing schools to improve.

Public school choice is not a new phenomenon. Prior to NCLB, there already existed an array of school choice arrangements across the nation. These included magnet schools, alternative schools, public charter schools, open-enrollment schools, and intra- and inter-district choice programs. Even before NCLB, almost every major city offered families more than one school to choose from, and the number of states allowing students to transfer to new schools inside or outside of their districts has increased steadily since the early 1990s. Nationally, the percentage of students enrolled in schools they had selected increased from 4.7 million students in 1993 to 6.9 million in 1999. Figures from that same period show that the percentage of schools allowing the enrollment of students who live outside the district grew from 26% to 46%.[10] The existing programs that most closely mirror NCLB-mandated choice are the intra-district choice programs that allow parents to choose among a set of district schools. Cities such as New York, Boston, and Boulder, Colorado, have long-standing intra-district choice programs. Even in districts without a formal intra-district channel, assertive parents have long been able to secure permission from district officials to enroll their students in non-neighborhood schools.

All the students at a Title I school deemed "in need of improvement" are to be given the option to transfer to another public school within the district or to a nearby charter school. How are districts to deal with these requests if the number of students seeking transfers exceeds the supply of seats in schools that are making AYP? According to a U.S. Department of Education regulation, districts are to find a way to expand the capacity of successful schools so as to create room for all students who want to attend. Lack of capacity is not considered a permissible excuse for failing to provide choice. Options for expanding capacity include adding classrooms or modular units to these schools, replicating the schools, and shifting to a year-round schedule in order to make space for more children. In reality, though, the lack of capacity in AYP-compliant schools is keeping thousands of eligible children from utilizing public school choice. In Chicago, for example, over 200,000 students were eligible for choice in 2005, over 20,000 expressed interest, but only a few thousand spaces were available. Other big cities faced similar constraints.

When it comes to transporting students for purposes of public school choice and supplemental services (discussed later in this chapter), districts are required to spend an amount equal to 20% of their Title I allocation for costs including transportation. If funds are tight, districts are to give priority to the lowest-achieving students from low-income families.

What happens if all of the elementary (or middle or high) schools in a district fail to make AYP? To which other school are eligible children supposed to transfer? Districts are required to try "to the extent practicable" to reach an agreement with other districts in order to ensure that their students have access to a better school outside of district borders. As of 2005, these agreements have been rare occurrences, as few districts have been interested in accepting new, needy students. Even if districts were, it is unclear whether the sending districts would be required to pay tuition to the receiving districts.

Another challenge for NCLB-style choice is convincing the principals of schools making AYP to cooperate by accepting students from low-performing schools. New arrivals from failing schools might drive test scores down in their new schools, making life more difficult for principals and teachers in schools that accept transfers. This creates a strong incentive for principals in these "receiving" schools to underestimate their available space, to avoid finding room for more students, and to generally find ways to limit the number of NCLB transfer students they will receive.

One other important limitation on NCLB choice is that districts are responsible for informing parents of their choice options, even though administrators can find disseminating this information and dealing with the transportation logistics of choice to be a headache. To make public school choice work, states are required to calculate and disseminate their schools' AYP ratings before the beginning of the school year. Districts must then notify parents, also before the first day of school, that their children are eligible for a transfer and provide them with a list of available schools. Unfortunately, AYP determinations are typically announced very late in the summer or even after the beginning of the new school year, throwing a big wrench into this design.[11] Furthermore, if information about choice options is scarce, the more motivated and alert parents are the only ones likely to take advantage of it; in a few places, this is exactly what is happening.

Public school choice was widely used before the passage of NCLB. As Richard Colvin of Columbia University Teachers College has noted, "The school choice provisions of NCLB represent . . . a minor adjustment to far more expansive school choice programs."[12] How did NCLB-style choice actually alter existing arrangements? Well, prior to NCLB, the vast majority of public school choice was nebulously linked to school improvement, with no specific effort to ensure that students in troubled schools were given a chance to transfer out. NCLB, for the first time, sought to explicitly link public school choice to the goal of improving student achievement. Rather than an escape hatch for a few disgruntled parents, NCLB-style choice is intended to be a systemic solution to a structural problem. Whether it will have the hoped-for effect remains an open question.

There is some evidence that a growing number of parents are seeking to take advantage of the public school choice provision; parental awareness of the opportunity may grow as the number of schools in improvement status increases. A 2004 report by the Citizens' Commission on Civil Rights found that approximately 70,000 students exercised public school choice in the 2003–2004 school year, though the requests for transfers far outpaced the number of actual transfers that took place. [13] For instance, the report pegged the percentage of eligible students who requested public school choice as growing from 2.3% in 2002–2003 to 6.2% in 2003–2004. Meanwhile, the percentage of those students who actually transferred was only 1.3% and 1.7%. The Commission report also found that the number of students requesting transfers varied from district to district and state to state. While Syracuse, New York, and Portland, Oregon, boasted that 20% of eligible students exercised NCLB choice, almost no students transferred in districts such as Worcester, Massachusetts, and Patterson, New Jersey.[14] Though systematic data are still hard to find, and though the situation is fluid, there is evidence that requests for NCLB transfers appear to be increasing with time.

Though it is not a part of the cascade of sanctions, it is important to note that schools can also encounter the public school choice sanction if they are deemed unsafe. NCLB has a "persistently dangerous schools" clause that asks each state to define a state standard for school safety. Using data on expulsions, suspensions, crime, violence, and parental input, states are supposed to identify schools that are "persistently dangerous" and offer students at those schools the option to transfer to another public school. In addition, individual students who are the victims of violent crime at school have the right to transfer. The handful of schools that have so far been deemed "persistently dangerous" has led to criticism that states aren't taking the "persistently dangerous" provision seriously. As of June 2004, only 38 schools nationwide had been defined as persistently dangerous and 46 states and the District of Columbia reported having no unsafe schools at all. However, while cities such as Los Angeles, Chicago, and Detroit claimed no persistently dangerous schools in 2003, Pennsylvania declared 27 public schools in Philadelphia to be unsafe.[15] Given these discrepancies, the Department of Education has urged states to create a more stringent definition of "persistently dangerous" schools.

Critics of school choice have long worried that parental choice will lead to stratification by social class, capable students fleeing troubled schools, racial segregation, and a reduced commitment to public education.[16] Those concerns, however, have been relatively muted with regard to the NCLB public choice provision and public choice programs in general and are far more prevalent when it comes to charter schooling or school voucher programs. Given the restrictions on who may exercise NCLB public choice (only students in "needs improvement" schools), the fact that all money remains squarely in public school district coffers, and general agreement that children in the most troubled schools are being ill served, there has been widespread support for the public choice provision, even among some liberals and progressives who are skeptical of more ambitious choice-based reforms. Concerns about the requirements have been most evident from school district administrators, many of whom regard the requirement as a distraction and a logistical headache, and who would at least like students to receive supplemental services before being given the chance to switch schools. In the fall of 2005 Secretary Spellings indicated a willingness to heed their concerns when she allowed four districts to offer supplemental services before public school choice on an experimental basis.

Supplemental Educational Services

If a Title I school fails to make AYP for a third consecutive year, it remains in improvement status, must continue to provide public school choice, and must also notify low-income parents that their chil-

**Supplemental
educational services**

offer free tutoring or other
additional academic help
outside the regular school
day

dren are now eligible for **supplemental educational services** (SES). SES is a provision that provides eligible students with free tutoring. A bit of context may be helpful before we fully explain SES.

School vouchers, which allow students to use public funding to attend the public or private school of their choice, have been a favored education reform for Republicans since the 1980s. The original NCLB blueprint contained a voucher provision for children in failing schools. It would have given students in these schools a $1,500 "exit voucher" to help them attend the public or private school of their choice. During negotiations, as was discussed in chapter 1, the voucher clause was dropped and public school choice and supplemental educational services were included in its stead.[17] The supplemental services provision was the more voucher-like replacement because it allowed parents to spend public money on a public or private provider of tutoring of their choice.[18]

Supplemental services can be provided in various ways and for varying amounts of time, depending on the providers that operate in a district and that parents choose to utilize. States are required to designate a list of approved supplemental services providers. While the approval criteria are largely left up to the states, in general, approved providers must have a proven track record of successful student tutoring and a sound financial status. The law explicitly demands that states cultivate as large and diverse a portfolio of providers as possible in order to give parents as many choices as possible. The list of approved providers can include for-profit and non-profit companies, community and faith-based organizations, teachers or teacher associations, and school districts. It rapidly became clear that the districts themselves would be the leading providers of tutoring, at least in the initial years of NCLB. In Chicago, for example, half of the 80,000 students receiving free tutoring in the 2004–2005 school year enrolled in the district's own program. Much of the money stayed within the system, softening the potential blow from lots of money flowing out of the school system to private providers.

Once the list of approved providers is set, districts are responsible for disseminating an annual notice to low-income parents about the availability of supplemental services, the names of providers that are available in the district, and a profile of each provider. Individual parents then choose an approved tutoring provider from the state list, and the district contracts with that organization. If requested, the district is also obligated to assist parents in selecting a provider. According to a federal study of supplemental services in nine districts, tutoring is typically offered two to three times a week immediately after school for an hour or two.[19] It generally costs the district between $1,000 and $2,000 per student. NCLB also stipulates that districts with schools in improvement status must set aside an amount equal to 20% of their Title I budget to pay for transportation costs related to school choice and for SES.

Approved providers are required to consult with the district and parents to formulate a student achievement plan that lays out specific goals, ways of measuring progress, and a timetable for improvement. Once tutoring has started, providers are responsible for ensuring that their content and instruction are in accord with state content standards, that their program is devoid of ideology or religion, and that they assess and report student progress. States are responsible for holding SES providers accountable for improving student achievement and are supposed to remove from the approved provider list those providers which fail to improve student achievement for two consecutive years.

The design of SES poses a couple of unusual challenges for policy-makers and educators. First, the districts that have become providers are placed in an awkward position. They are expected to facilitate the free tutoring that other organizations are providing, by informing parents and negotiating contracts and the like, while also competing with these organizations as rival providers. This scenario has been likened by some to a "fox guarding the henhouse."[20] This issue is somewhat mitigated by a Department of Education regulation that bars districts that are "in need of improvement" from serving as providers themselves; by 2005 most large urban districts had entered this status. However, in the fall of 2005, Secretary Spellings relaxed this regulation and allowed a number of "needs improvement" districts, including Chicago, New York City, and Boston, to serve as providers.

A second potential problem relates to accountability for providers, which is largely left up to the states. States are expected to determine how providers will measure and report student improvement, how much progress will be enough, and which providers will be removed from the approved list. Of course, state officials do not have much time, expertise, or motivation to address these tasks, raising questions about how successfully they will weed out ineffective providers.

Corrective Action

Districts can choose to take corrective action at any time if they decide that a school is in need of dramatic improvement, but they must take corrective action if a school fails to make AYP for a fourth consecutive year. Schools that fail to make AYP for a fourth consecutive year continue to offer public school choice and supplemental services but are also subject to additional, more intense interventions. The law states that corrective action must involve at least one of the following steps:

- implement a new curriculum based on state standards and conduct professional development for all personnel involved
- decrease management authority at the school
- replace some school employees
- appoint outside experts to run the school
- extend the school day and/or school year
- restructure the organization of the school.

Once the district formulates a corrective action

plan, it must publish and disseminate the content of that plan to the parents of the children in that school and to the public through the Internet, the media, and public agencies.

The law gives districts a choice with regard to which corrective action to take, and it would not be surprising if most districts opted for the least disruptive and most palatable actions. A change in curriculum or an extension of the school day is far less messy than replacing the staff or restructuring internal arrangements. Of particular importance is the fact that existing **collective bargaining agreements** remain in effect during corrective action. This means that districts may be unable to implement drastic staffing changes or internal reorganizations and might have difficulty extending the school day or year. To date, there is little reliable evidence on how aggressively districts are moving when it comes to corrective action plans or what these plans tend to look like.

Collective bargaining agreements

contracts between employers and labor unions

Restructuring

The final and most extensive remedy for failing schools is "restructuring," a set of major interventions intended to change the governance arrangements of these schools in order to stimulate improvement. The rationale is that some schools have been so dysfunctional for so long that only a "fresh start" will succeed in turning things around. Schools that fail to make AYP for a fifth consecutive year must develop a restructuring plan, and that plan must be implemented no later than the beginning of the next school year. Districts must plan and implement at least one of five possible restructuring options identified in the law. These include:

- reopening the school as a charter school
- replacing all or most of the school staff (including the principal)
- contracting with a private entity such as an **educational management organization (EMO)** with a history of effective school management
- arranging for a state takeover

Educational management organizations (EMOs)

companies providing management and administrative services to some public schools

- restructuring school governance in accord with state direction
- undertaking any other major restructuring of the school's governance that produces fundamental reform.

NCLB's restructuring requirements represent serious and far-reaching governance changes. Though some are more extensive than others, on the whole these required actions are not cosmetic changes to curriculum, staffing, or service delivery, but major structural overhauls of schools. At the same time, the final restructuring option mentioned—"some other restructuring of school governance"—is written loosely enough that states or districts not interested in making significant changes might use it as a loophole to maintain the status quo.

These restructuring options had been attempted at failing schools across the country before NCLB with mixed results. Though there are few systematic studies of conversion charters, it is not surprising that limited observational evidence suggests that simply changing the governance of a failing school without accompanying efforts to address personnel, organization, or instruction may have only a limited impact on student achievement.

One alternative to charter "conversions" is to disband and replace failing schools. In such a process, failing schools are essentially dissolved and replaced in the same building by new schools, which can either be district schools or charter schools. The "fresh start" approach calls for these new schools to hire different principals, make substantial staffing changes, and implement a wholesale reform plan.[21] Some observers have raised doubts as to how much of a fresh start this approach actually entails, or whether the new schools—especially if they are traditional district schools—may prove to be little more than the same school with a new principal and improvement plan. NCLB does not provide any direction as to which remedies states should prefer.

The restructuring provision also references two other potential reforms: contracting the school to an

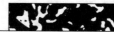

educational management organization (EMO) and a takeover by the state. The education management sector has grown rapidly since the mid-1990s. EMOs are organizations, typically for-profit, which manage a chain of schools much as traditional districts manage their schools. The longest-established EMO, Edison Schools, was only launched in 1992; by 2003, there were nearly 50 such organizations managing more than 400 schools in 24 states. Various studies have sought to determine whether EMOs systematically outperform traditionally managed schools. To date, the record of education management organizations (EMOs) in promoting student achievement and school improvement is mixed. Some studies, for instance, have found that EMO-run charter schools post larger gains than other charter schools.[22] Other research has suggested that EMOs do not outperform similar public schools or has raised questions about the ability of for-profit firms to improve student achievement while turning a profit.[23]

With regard to state or mayoral takeovers, most research on the impact of these measures has been conducted at the district level. As of 2004, 29 states allowed for state or city takeover of public school districts, and takeovers have occurred in 18 states and Washington, DC.[24] In 2004, 23 states also had policies that would allow state takeover of individual schools, though only two states had utilized the provision by that year. As of 2004, seven states had mandated school **reconstitution** for their worst schools, often putting the onus on districts to manage the reconstitution and improvement efforts.[25] Overall, takeovers have yielded mixed results at the district level, and there is little research on state takeover of individual schools. As with all of NCLB's restructuring remedies, takeovers are unlikely to prove "a silver bullet solution."[26]

A study of NCLB-prompted school restructuring in Michigan by the Center on Education Policy provided some early evidence on how restructuring works in practice. During 2004–2005, 133 schools in Michigan—5% of the state's schools—were in restructuring status. The vast majority were located in urban

Reconstitution
a drastic corrective action for a school whose students have continually performed poorly; reconstitution involves replacement of most of the school's staff and faculty

areas, with over 50% in the Detroit area alone. Michigan's restructuring options are similar to those provided by NCLB, though state takeover is not an option and schools are permitted to implement an external, research-based reform plan or hire a "coach" from the state's "Coaches Institute for High Priority Schools." Seventy-eight of the restructuring schools replaced staff and/or the principal, while 22 appointed a "coach" from the "Coaches Institute" and 19 appointed an independent turnaround specialist. Other, more disruptive changes, were much less popular. Not a single school had decided to become a charter school, turn school management over to a private management company, or extend the school day or school year.[27]

District Accountability

NCLB also extends its cascading remedies to entire school districts. Any school district that fails to make AYP for two consecutive years is labeled "in need of improvement" and must develop an improvement plan within three months of being so identified. Among other things, the improvement plan must:

- dedicate no less than 10% of Title I funding to teacher professional development
- delineate measurable goals for each subgroup
- include plans for after school programs, summer enrichment, and the extension of the school year
- lay out the roles of the state education agency and the district in the improvement plan
- develop strategies to increase parental involvement.

Once formulated, the improvement plan must be implemented no later than the beginning of the following school year. The state education agency is responsible for offering technical assistance to failing districts in implementing their improvement plans, especially when it comes to professional development and parental involvement.

Once a district is deemed in need of improvement,

the state agency may take corrective action at any time. If the improvement plan fails to help the district make AYP for two more consecutive years, the state is required to take corrective action. The corrective actions suggested for districts are slightly different from those suggested for schools. States must choose one of the following corrective actions:

- defer programmatic funds or reduce administrative funds
- implement a new curriculum
- replace personnel
- remove certain schools from the jurisdiction of the district and place them under "alternative governance arrangements"
- appoint a trustee to replace the superintendent and board of education
- abolish or restructure the district
- authorize students in the failing district to transfer to a high-performing school in another district.

While many schools were "in need of improvement" under the old ESEA statute prior to 2001, few districts were so identified before the 2004–2005 school year. As a result, during 2005–2006 the implementation of this provision was just starting to take shape. It remains to be seen whether states are willing to take decisive "corrective" action in their failing districts, how they will proceed, and how effective these efforts will be.

Conclusion

The assessment, accountability, and choice provisions are at the heart of No Child Left Behind. While they take up only a small percentage of the law's hundreds of pages, they form the foundation of the act. For the most part, these are the policies that have led some reformers to hail NCLB as a landmark law and critics to condemn it as a case of federal overreaching.

To recap, NCLB requires that all public schools annually test all their students in grades 3 through 8 in reading and math (and once in high school), and that every state measure whether its public schools are making "adequate yearly progress" (AYP) toward universal proficiency in these core subjects. States will also be required to begin testing students in science in the 2007–2008 school year, though those results will not count toward AYP. Each school and each school district must meet rising expectations for a variety of subgroups. Schools are evaluated on the achievement level of each subgroup, so long as the group exceeds a state-determined minimum size. Schools or districts which fail to "make AYP" in any of those categories in either reading or math for two years in a row are judged to be "in need of improvement" and subject to a cascade of sanctions and interventions that grow more draconian with each additional year of failure.

In the early stages of intervention, NCLB stresses alternatives for children in these faltering schools, aiming both to provide these students with an escape hatch and to create incentives for the schools to improve. If a federally aided school fails to make AYP for two consecutive years, students are to be offered public school choice, and the school must develop an improvement plan. If a school fails to improve in subsequent years, the district must offer low-income students free tutoring, known as supplemental education services (SES). Finally, if the school still hasn't improved after five years, it is to be "restructured" in various ways. Districts are also subject to their own cascade of state interventions, triggered by the failure of students district-wide to meet the AYP benchmarks. These processes are to be designed by the states, in accord with NCLB guidelines.

On paper, this all proceeds in an orderly fashion, with federal regulations telling states what to do, states telling districts what to do, and local school systems charged with improving low-performing schools and providing options to students. State education departments are charged with setting standards, creating tests, intervening in districts that don't make AYP, and so on. That hierarchy of responsibility—from Washington to state capital to local

school system—has been around for decades, but was never designed to support a performance-based accountability system or to improve low-performing schools. Many of the challenges we are witnessing today are due to a grand experiment—namely, whether the complicated machinery of NCLB and the old machinery of American education will mesh in the manner that Congress intended.

We will now turn to NCLB's effort to improve teacher quality before considering the law's provisions regarding research, reading, and a variety of other policies and programs. It is the accountability system at the heart of NCLB, though, more than any other component of the law, that has changed the ways states, school districts, educators, and parents think and talk about schooling.

GLOSSARY

Adequate yearly progress (AYP)—is the minimum level of improvement that schools and school districts must make each year, as determined under the NCLB Act and related state rules. Each state specifies and sets measurable objectives for all of its schools and districts, which must lead to 100% proficiency in reading and math by 2013–2014. Failure to achieve AYP two years in a row results in sanctions for schools and districts, with sanctions growing more severe over time.

Collective bargaining agreements—the contracts between an employer and a labor union. They determine wages, hours, rules, and working conditions. Most teachers are employed under a collective bargaining agreement that is negotiated with the local school district.

Disaggregation—means to separate a whole into its parts. In the case of NCLB accountability, it involves separating average test results into various groups of students. The law requires holding schools and districts accountable for the achievement of groups of students who are economically disadvantaged, from each racial and ethnic group, have disabilities, or have limited English proficiency. This practice allows parents and teachers to see how each group of students is performing.

Educational management organizations (EMOs)—are private, for-profit companies some public schools (especially charter schools) use for management and administrative purposes.

In need of improvement schools—are schools that receive Title I funds yet fail to make adequate yearly progress (AYP) for two straight years. These schools are required to develop a plan to improve student achievement, and districts are to provide these schools with additional support and resources. Students in these schools become eligible for public school choice after two years and for supplemental educational services if the school fails to make AYP for a third consecutive year.

Levels of achievement—are the different levels that measure a student's mastery of material, specifically the mastery of reading, mathematics, and, beginning in 2007–2008, science, such as "basic," "proficient," and "advanced."

National Assessment of Educational Progress (NAEP)—An independent benchmark, NAEP is the only nationally representative and continuing assessment of what American students know and can do in various subject areas. Since 1969, the National Center for Education Statistics has conducted NAEP assessments in reading, mathematics, science, writing, U.S. history, civics, geography, and the arts.

Public school choice—Title I schools that do not make adequate yearly progress for two consecutive years, which are labeled in need of improvement, must offer all students the opportunity to transfer to another public school in their district or to a local charter school. The school district is required to pay for transportation for the students, and if not enough funds are available, priority must be given to low-income students.

Reconstitution—drastic corrective action for a school whose students have performed poorly for several years and have failed to improve. A reconstitution is marked by the replacement of the majority of the school's staff, the hiring of a new principal, and the re-staffing of its faculty from scratch. Only a few school districts have adopted this method of reform.

Safe harbor—a provision in No Child Left Behind that is intended for schools and districts that are making progress in student achievement but are not yet meeting target goals for adequate yearly progress (AYP). It is designed to prevent the over-identification of schools not making AYP.

School improvement plan—the written plan for each Title I school deemed in need of improvement; it includes strategies for improving student performance, taking into account the performance on multiple assessments; how and when improvements will be implemented; and use of state funds. Each school improvement plan must be approved by the local school board and may be in effect for no more than three years.

Subgroup—a small group of students separated from the whole group that may be present in a school or school system. The subgroups specified under the NCLB law are Native American/Alaskan Native students, Asian/Pacific Islander students, Black students, white students, Hispanic students, students with limited English proficiency, students who are economically disadvantaged, and students with disabilities.

Supplemental educational services—are free tutoring services or additional academic help provided outside of the regular school day. These services are generally available to low-income students in Title I schools that have failed to make AYP for three consecutive years. Parents of these students can choose from a list of state-approved supplemental service providers, and the expenses are covered by the districts, generally with federal funds.

Universal proficiency—is the end goal of NCLB. The law's aim is to make 100% of the nation's students proficient in mathematics and English by the school year 2013–2014 as determined by tests. This goal is much more ambitious than universal access, a goal the nation has achieved by ensuring that all students—regardless of race, immigrant status, or disability—have access to the public schools.

Value-added—measures a student's performance from the beginning of a school year to the end, thus demonstrating the influence a school has on a student's academic performance. This reporting provides diagnostic information for improving education opportunities for students at all achievement levels.

CHAPTER THREE

The Highly Qualified Teacher Provision

Federal mandate

a command issued by the federal government requiring that private organizations, states, or local governments implement certain federal rules or decisions

After its accountability and choice provisions, NCLB's most significant departure from existing policy was the **federal mandate** that all children be taught by a "highly qualified teacher" by the end of the 2005–2006 school year. While such a requirement may sound commonsensical, it amounted to an enormous expansion of the federal government's involvement in education policies that had once been left to the states. Why the emphasis on teacher quality in a law focused upon testing and accountability?

As teacher quality advocate Kati Haycock argued in 2002, "New research makes it clear that teachers have the single greatest effect on student learning. Students who have several effective, well-prepared teachers in a row have the best chance to soar, while students who have even two ineffective teachers in a row are unlikely to ever recover."[1] Meanwhile, observers of all stripes agreed with veteran educators Vivian Troen's and Katherine Boles's 2003 contention that existing "certification requirements are nearly irrelevant" and fail to "prevent poorly prepared or unqualified teachers from entering the [nation's] classrooms."[2] While reformers disagreed on the appropriate solution, they agreed on the problem.

While the assessment and accountability provisions of NCLB were largely consistent with the principles that George W. Bush had campaigned on in 2000 and with the blueprint he proposed in 2001, the story is very different with regard to the bill's much-discussed "highly qualified teacher" provision. This provision was absent from Bush's campaign promises and from the first draft of NCLB. In contrast to the assessment and accountability provisions, which were born of widespread agreement between Republicans and centrist "New Democrats," the highly qualified teacher language was championed by liberal Representative George Miller of California. The highest-ranking Democrat on the House Education and the Workforce Committee, Miller supported the NCLB assessment and accountability provisions but also believed that the federal government had to focus on teacher quality if schools were to have any chance of reaching the new expectations. Returning to a theme raised in the early years of President Clinton's administration, Miller insisted that the federal government focus not only on student outcomes but on ensuring that all students have good teachers and an "opportunity to learn."

Historically, school districts have struggled with a well-documented shortage of such "qualified" teachers, especially when staffing schools that serve the most disadvantaged children. In 1997, the U.S. Department of Education reported that 25% of all new teachers were hired without the "proper qualifications." This finding was particularly noteworthy given that "proper qualifications" typically referred to required coursework rather than proof of competence or teaching ability. The numbers were even more distressing for urban districts, where more than 75% of new teachers lacked the requisite qualifications. In effect, the research documented a "teacher quality gap" between rich and poor schools, one that mirrors the achievement gap between different groups of students.[3] Because the certification and hiring of teachers was left entirely to states and local school districts, the federal government played almost no role in addressing this issue. The Highly Qualified Teacher provision was significant because it overturned this tenet of **federalism** and gave the federal government an active role in improving teacher quality.

Federalism

a form of government in which multiple levels of government have formal authority over the same land, area, and people

The Highly Qualified Teacher (HQT) provision was designed to address the teacher quality gap, in an effort to help close the student achievement gap. It sought to take away the discretion of local school districts to hire unqualified teachers and push states to place a higher priority on teachers' subject matter knowledge. The law constitutes the single most aggressive and far-reaching act at the federal level to improve teacher quality, even while remaining relatively vague about just what "highly qualified" means.

What Is a "Highly Qualified" Teacher?

Core academic subjects

The core academic subjects are English, reading/language arts, mathematics, science, foreign languages, civics and government, economics, art, history, and geography.

Under NCLB's regulations, all teachers of **core academic subjects** must be highly qualified by the end of the 2005–2006 school year. The core subjects are: English, reading/language arts, mathematics, science, foreign languages, civics and government, economics, arts, history, and geography. To be "highly qualified," a teacher must hold a bachelor's degree, have obtained a state teaching certification or passed the state teacher licensing examination, and have demonstrated knowledge of the subject that he or she teaches. Teachers must also not have "had certification or licensure requirements waived on an emergency, temporary, or provisional basis."[4] What is required for certification, how rigorous a licensing exam should be, or what constitutes sufficient content knowledge is—as with the content of standards—left to the states themselves.

In fact, much of this ambiguity was intentional, given the heated debate surrounding the issue of teacher quality. While everyone agrees that teacher quality is the most important school-based factor in affecting student achievement, there is sharp disagreement about what makes for a highly qualified teacher and how we can hire more of them. Framing this debate is the frustrating fact that there "does not appear to be a strong link between many readily quantifiable teacher attributes . . . and teacher quality."[5] In other words, though there is widespread agreement that good teachers matter, there is less agreement about the training, credentials, or qualities that make a good teacher.

Given the absence of rigorous research on teacher quality, it is perhaps not surprising that a heated debate has emerged about the value of requiring teachers to complete training programs or obtain state credentials. The proponents of conventional licensure, including most of the leading figures from the world of teacher education, assert that formal preparation at a college of education and state certification are the best predictors of teaching success. Critics, most of them housed outside of education schools, argue that traditional preparation is not as important as academic proficiency and on-the-job experience in predicting teacher quality. Despite the discord, several broad, generally agreed-upon findings helped to shape NCLB's teacher quality provision.

There is a general consensus that the most effective teachers have a high level of "academic proficiency." Researchers have measured "academic proficiency" or "general cognitive ability" in a number of different ways, from performance on licensure exams to the selectivity of a teacher's undergraduate institution to "verbal ability," as defined by a short vocabulary test. For instance, a comprehensive survey of research on teacher quality noted that the selectivity of a teacher's undergraduate institution is linked to the achievement of that teacher's students and that "the most consistent finding is that effective teachers score higher on tests of verbal ability and other standardized tests."[6]

With regard to content knowledge, several studies have suggested that math and science teachers with deeper knowledge of their subjects are more effective at the secondary level. There is little research, however, on how teacher content knowledge affects student achievement in English or social studies in secondary schools or at the elementary level.[7]

Most of the research on the effects of teacher experience shows that while beginning teachers are less effective than experienced teachers at boosting student achievement, a teacher's effectiveness grows considerably during his or her first few years in the profession. Simply put, no matter how strong their preparation, most new teachers struggle during their first one or two years in the classroom. After a teacher's first four or five years, however, the value of additional experience is much less clear. Scholars disagree on whether experience past the first five years leads to any predictable increase in effectiveness, and some research suggests that teachers with 20 or more years of experience are actually less effective than those with less time in the classroom.[8]

The research on how teacher preparation and licensure relate to teacher quality is largely inconclusive. The literature on the effectiveness of licensed versus non-licensed or emergency-credentialed teachers is "sparse and often methodologically flawed" and therefore "too weak to support strong conclusions."[9] As a result of this dearth of good research, state education agencies have little concrete guidance on who should be allowed to teach and what kind of system would best produce qualified candidates.[10]

State Standards for Teacher Quality Before NCLB

The lack of conclusive evidence with regard to teacher licensure and its effects on student achievement is unsurprising, given the tremendous variety of licensure arrangements that exist across the states. Until the late nineteenth century, the licensing and hiring of teachers was traditionally the duty of the local school board and superintendent. As the "common school" movement expanded over the course of the nineteenth century, enrollment in public schools grew considerably, increasing demand for educated individuals who could teach the burgeoning population of students. Local systems and, increasingly, state governments began to set qualifications for teachers in order to ensure competent hiring.

Slowly, in the early twentieth century, states developed education agencies and partnered with budding schools of education in an effort to standardize teacher preparation and licensure. Starting in the 1950s, this "educational establishment" was joined by groups representing classroom teachers, like teachers unions and professional associations, each desiring to "professionalize" teaching in certain ways and equipped with particular notions of how teacher licensure systems should be structured. The general trend was a shift toward state control over teacher certification, but states approached this development in various ways.[11]

While every state mandates that public school teachers obtain a teaching license, most also include provisions for "emergency" certificates that allow non-licensed individuals to teach if no certified teachers are available. Some states also exempt charter school teachers from certification requirements. Almost all states require that prospective teachers complete a teacher preparation program at an approved and accredited college or university.[12] However, by 2002, 46 states had an "alternative licensure" program that enabled individuals to enter the teaching profession from non-traditional backgrounds and without attendance at a college of education. The number of alternative certification programs has increased rapidly since the early 1980s, and alternatively licensed teachers today make up nearly 10% of the national teaching corps. In 2005, alternatively licensed teachers accounted for 35,000 teachers, or nearly 20% of those entering the profession.[13]

The majority of teachers, then, obtain their certification through "traditional" routes. But what does this traditional system look like? Again, apart from a consistent core of requirements, the systems vary by state. As of 2004, all states required a bachelor's degree and some training in pedagogy. Forty-two states required high school teachers to have coursework in their subjects. In 46 states, prospective teachers were required to take a certification test, though eight states tested only basic skills and most tests were pegged at a twelfth-grade level or below.[14]

Within this common core there is much diversity. Some states set very prescriptive requirements for licensure. For instance, Louisiana has a set number of hours in pedagogy courses that all teachers must complete. Other states give individual teacher-training programs a great deal of discretion in coursework and other requirements. Indiana and North Carolina indicate the topics that must be taught but leave the course requirements and the distribution of instructional time to the colleges and universities.

These arrangements have come under increasing scrutiny. On one hand, proponents of "professionalization," including the colleges of education, national teachers unions, professional teachers associations, and collaborative efforts like the National Commission for Teaching and America's Future have pushed for more formal training and longer internships for teacher candidates, accreditation of teacher preparation programs by the National Council for the Accreditation of Teacher Education, and increased professional development. The hallmark of this "professionalization" approach is the desire to ensure "control of the profession by professional educators who understand the unique skills of teaching."[15] This camp, while willing to rethink the old system, has been largely successful in resisting attempts to implement broad reform of the teacher certification apparatus.

On the other hand, mediocre student achievement and an impending teacher shortage in some areas have prompted some critics to question whether the existing system attracts and produces the best possible teaching candidates. These advocates call for deregulation of the teaching profession, reduction of licensure barriers, more consideration of nontraditional candidates, and increased principal discretion in hiring. Groups such as the National Council on Teacher Quality and the American Board for

Certification of Teacher Excellence have emerged to push this alternative agenda.[16]

In the 1990s, owing to a booming economy and flush budgets, many states were able to implement expensive professionalism initiatives. Such reforms included across the board pay raises, financial incentives for nationally certified master teachers, and increased funding to teacher preparation programs. By 2004, 46 states had partnered with the National Council for Accreditation of Teacher Education (NCATE), and 29 provided bonuses to teachers certified by the National Board for Professional Teaching Standards. At the same time, starting in the 1990s, many states expanded alternative certification routes in an effort to alleviate teacher shortages, though alternative certification remains tightly regulated in most states and often entails the same coursework requirements as traditional licensure.[17]

Federal Efforts Before NCLB

The teacher quality reforms of the 1990s coincided with increased activism on the part of the federal government. Because teacher preparation and licensure had always been a state function, the federal government traditionally practiced a hands-off approach. As national interest in public education grew through the 1960s and 1970s, and after the 1983 release of *A Nation at Risk,* the federal government slowly began to delve into teacher quality issues. Importantly, however, even the most involved federal initiatives have always assumed the governance of teacher preparation and certification to be a state responsibility.

The federal government's first foray into teacher quality was part of the National Defense Education Act of 1958 (NDEA). The Soviet Union's launch of the *Sputnik* satellite panicked Americans and fueled concerns that the nation's failure to invest in math and science education was to blame for its falling behind in the space race. Congress responded with the NDEA, a law that included dramatic increases in federal funding for teacher preparation in mathematics and science. It included provisions to defer or forgive college loans for aspiring teachers of math, science, or a foreign language and earmarked $1 billion over four years for teacher professional development in these target subjects. In 1964, the law was amended to include funding for teacher training in the humanities.[18]

President Lyndon Johnson's Great Society agenda launched the next wave of federal teacher quality legislation. The original ESEA and the Higher Education Act (HEA) of 1965 both included teacher quality provisions. ESEA dedicated funds to in-service teacher training and, later, to preservice professional development for aspiring teachers. The HEA set up the revolutionary Teacher Corps program, which was designed to train prospective teachers for the challenges of urban schooling.

The 1983 release of *A Nation at Risk* re-ignited the push for greater federal involvement in education, but the teacher quality initiatives of the mid-1980s did not amount to much. In 1985, the American Defense Education Act cited reports of a looming teacher shortage in math and science and exhorted education schools to partner with school districts to provide professional development. However, one expert summarized the efforts of the 1980s by noting, "While reports of teacher shortages in areas such as mathematics and physics were much cited, little was done beyond continued investment in teacher in-service training."[19]

The standards and accountability movement that began in the early 1990s turned a spotlight onto teachers, sparking new efforts to attract and develop quality faculty. By the mid-1990s, teacher quality was a recurring theme in discussions of standards. A 1996 report by the National Commission on Teaching and America's Future (NCTAF)—an assemblage of education reformers, education college professors, business leaders, and union members—declared that the status quo system of recruiting, preparing, and developing teachers was not up to the new challenges of standards-based accountability. The NCTAF report advocated an overhaul of teacher education, standards for certification, and teacher recruitment.[20]

These sentiments were echoed in both houses of Congress in the 1998 reauthorization of the Higher Education Act (HEA). That year, Democratic Representative George Miller of California and Senator Jeff Bingaman, a Democrat from New Mexico, managed to insert into Title II of HEA two separate acts that increased accountability for teachers and teacher preparation programs. The new Title II mandated that colleges and universities issue an annual report to their state on the quality of their preparation programs and on the pass rates of their teacher candidates on licensure assessments. The states would then have to report these findings to the U.S. Department of Education, which would compile the reports and pass them on to Congress and the public. The states were also charged with developing criteria for deeming schools of education "low performing," and for applying these criteria and intervening with assistance and sanctions as appropriate.[21]

By attempting to extend accountability to teacher preparation, the 1998 reauthorization of HEA marked a departure from the traditional federal role. The change spawned criticism from education schools and some minorities activists. Education schools were naturally reluctant to be held accountable for their candidates, asserting that any blame should also fall on their sister academic departments and arguing that evaluating programs on the basis of a licensure assessment was unreasonable and unfair. Some minority advocacy groups worried that holding education schools accountable for the performance of graduates on licensure exams would discourage these institutions from recruiting minorities. They also feared that such a policy would have an adverse impact on historically black colleges and universities.

Though Congress passed the Title II amendments over opposition from these groups, the new provisions of HEA did not work as designed. The Education Trust reported, "Many states simply did not answer the questions about low performance or reported criteria so vague or timelines so long that one had to wonder whether there was any intention to act."[22] Much of the data in the first report, compiled in 2001 and released in 2002, "was inconsistent, incomplete, and utterly incomprehensible."[23] Several years later, the provisions have yet to deliver the hoped-for results.

Crafting the NCLB "Highly Qualified Teacher" Provision

In 2001, Representative Miller, the ranking Democratic member on the House Education Committee, had long been a staunch advocate for improving teacher quality. He also enjoyed a cordial personal relationship with Republican John Boehner of Ohio, the Chairman of the House Education and the Workforce Committee. As NCLB was working its way through Congress, in an effort to help ensure the legislation had wide bipartisan backing, Boehner gave Miller the lead in drafting the law's teacher quality provision. After all, it was not a top Republican priority—the term "highly qualified teacher" did not appear in President Bush's original NCLB proposal.

Miller and his staff worked closely with Education Trust, the liberal advocacy group, to craft provisions reflecting their concern that states had not set tough enough requirements for subject matter knowledge. They sought to dramatically strengthen the federal government's hand in improving teacher quality. Their original proposal would have set the same rigorous requirements for new teachers and veterans: a college degree, full state certification, and demonstration of subject matter mastery by either passing a test or having a major in their taught subjects.

The proposal that veteran teachers be required to pass a test was anathema to the nation's teachers unions, especially its largest, the National Education Association (NEA). Arguing that such a "teacher testing" requirement would lead to teacher-bashing and a mass exodus of teachers from the nation's public schools, the NEA worked to convince Senator Ted

Kennedy, an influential veteran Massachusetts Democrat and longtime ally of the NEA, to push for a less stringent provision. Therefore, the final "highly qualified teacher" provision grew out of a compromise—not so much between Democrats and Republicans or liberals and conservatives but between two staunchly liberal Democratic members of Congress.

Remember, to be "highly qualified" under NCLB, a teacher must hold a bachelor's degree, have obtained state teaching certification or passed the state teacher licensing examination, and have demonstrated knowledge of the subject that he or she teaches. Because of the Miller-Kennedy compromise, these requirements are significantly different for new teachers than for veteran teachers. All new *elementary* teachers are required to have at least a bachelor's degree, be licensed by the state, and pass a rigorous state test proving their subject knowledge and teaching skills in the basic elementary areas including reading, writing, and mathematics. All new *middle and high school* teachers must have at least a bachelor's degree and a state teaching license. They must also either pass a rigorous state academic test in each subject they teach or have an academic major, coursework equivalent to a graduate degree, advanced certification, or credentialing in each subject they teach.

The selection or creation of a "rigorous state academic test" was left up to individual states, as was the definition of an academic major. In 2000–2001, the year before the adoption of NCLB, five states did not test elementary teachers at all. More generally, 21 states did not test for basic skills; 21 states did not test for subject matter; 27 did not test for pedagogical skills, and 46 had no performance assessment.[24] While NCLB led to the testing of more teacher candidates, it is not clear how rigorous the tests are or how seriously states have taken the requirements. In fact, as we discuss later in this chapter, these new mandates may have given states the incentive to actually reduce the difficulty of existing tests.

Requirements for Veteran Teachers

In order to ensure that *all* classrooms are staffed by highly qualified teachers, NCLB also requires veteran teachers to achieve highly qualified status. This was a tricky proposition, as it would have required states to tell veteran teachers, some with over 20 years of experience, that they were not "highly qualified" because they had not passed a test or because, decades ago, they did not take sufficient college courses in the area they now taught. After much pressure from the NEA and the active involvement of Senator Kennedy, Congress adopted a modified version of the highly qualified requirements for veteran teachers.

Like all new teachers, veteran teachers must have a bachelor's degree, be licensed by the state, and demonstrate subject matter competency. Also, like new teachers, they can demonstrate subject matter competency by passing a test or having a major in the subjects they teach. However, unlike new teachers, veteran teachers are given a third way to demonstrate their subject mastery. States were given the freedom to develop a "high objective uniform state standard of evaluation" **(HOUSSE)** to evaluate teachers' content mastery. The design of the HOUSSE model was left up to each state, but the Department recommended that some combination of college credits, advanced credentials, teaching experience, professional development, and student achievement. In other words, HOUSSE defines a set of experiences that can count toward demonstrating subject matter competence.

HOUSSE

a method to assess teachers' qualifications as an alternative to traditional methods

According to the U.S. Department of Education, most states' HOUSSE standards include one of five general categories: professional development, performance evaluation, classroom experience, a portfolio, and student achievement record. Some states, like Arkansas and Nevada, use only professional development, while some use only performance evaluation, like Florida, Washington, and West Virginia. Thirty states currently use a point system that incorporates two or more of these elements to satisfy the HOUSSE provision.[25] In a point system, the state defines a list of activities, each of which carries a certain number of points that count toward highly qualified status.

In New Jersey, for example, a teacher must accrue a total of ten points to be deemed "highly qualified." A college class completed in the subject area is worth two points, and with five classes a veteran teacher is considered "highly qualified." Certain professional activities are worth one point each. These include service on curriculum committees, professional development, content-area presentations, and interdisciplinary teaching with a content area specialist. Finally, veteran teachers with more than eight years of experience are awarded points for their years of teaching. Two points are accrued for eight to fifteen years, and three points for sixteen or more years of experience in the district, regardless of the teacher's student performance.[26] Critics have pointed out that the point system in many states is a meaningless paper exercise because the number of HOUSSE options "is too many for a district to responsibly oversee."[27]

The rigor of HOUSSE provisions varies from state to state. For example, Colorado requires all teachers to either pass a test in the subject they teach or complete coursework that is equivalent to a college major, while seven states grant highly qualified status to all veteran teachers who receive a satisfactory evaluation from their superiors. Alabama, Pennsylvania, Kansas, Maryland, and Hawaii mandate that all of their teachers have a minor in the subject they teach, but eleven states have declared that their certification system fulfills the highly qualified mandate on its own and requires no adjustments to fulfill NCLB. The National Council on Teacher Quality has argued that such a strategy may be acceptable for states with high certification standards, such as Idaho, but it is problematic in states with lax standards. Furthermore, some of these state policies appear to be in violation of the letter and spirit of the law; whether the U.S. Department of Education will intervene in those cases remains to be seen.

Some scholars have argued that the flexibility built into the HOUSSE provision threatens to derail the goal of the highly qualified teacher provision. Stanford University professor Terry Moe has charged, "The HOUSSE provisions create a loophole big enough to drive three million veteran teachers through— and the states have incentives to do just that."[28] States have little incentive to require their veteran teachers to obtain a subject area degree or subject them to a difficult exam; doing so would only aggravate the powerful teachers unions. Consequently, Moe asserted in 2004 that states are not setting high HOUSSE standards to ensure competence but are requiring very little of veteran teachers, opting for "self-assessments," additional professional development, or a supervisor evaluation rather than a rigorous exam of content knowledge. According to Moe, this state of affairs is tantamount to "making a mockery of the law and ensuring that incompetent and mediocre teachers will not be weeded out."[29]

The National Council on Teacher Quality has suggested that many states' HOUSSE provisions are plagued by such shortcomings. Reports in 2003 and 2004 by NCTQ identified six common problems in state HOUSSE standards. First, many states have offered teachers a large menu of ways to fulfill the standards, diluting their quality. Some states, like Michigan, made their HOUSSE provisions "inordinately complex," confusing teachers and administrators.[30] Second, some states have granted candidates subject-matter credit for irrelevant activities. For example, California, Michigan, and West Virginia have elected to give veteran teachers HOUSSE credit for applying for national board certification, regardless of whether they win approval.[31] Third, at least eight states have agreed to give HOUSSE credit for courses taken in the past, meaning that a teacher in Wyoming with three undergraduate math credits—not nearly enough for a major—can be declared highly qualified, while a new teacher with the same number of credits would be denied highly qualified status.[32] Fourth, a number of states have attached equal value to manifestly unequal activities. For instance, in Georgia, it was determined that teachers can obtain subject matter credit for having a doctoral degree in their field (quite impressive) or for attending two conferences (not so impressive). Fifth, there are a variety of loopholes in the HOUSSE processes established by most states. In New York, a teacher can obtain subject matter credit for supervising a student teacher, an option that could encourage weak teachers to volunteer for this critical role. Finally, some states have simply reframed their existing practices in order to fulfill NCLB's mandate: Idaho, for example, explained that the state certification system already took content knowledge into account, thereby precluding the need for a separate HOUSSE standard. The huge variety in the rigor of these standards raises questions about the value in even applying the HOUSSE requirements to veteran teachers in the first place. Undoubtedly, it is much harder for new teachers to earn highly qualified status than for veteran teachers.

Requirements for Paraprofessionals

NCLB also includes requirements for "paraprofessionals" (teacher aides) in Title I schools. Historically, a large proportion of Title I funds have supported the salaries of these aides, who are typically high-school educated mothers of children in the school. While these assistants provide key services, reformers were concerned that they were performing duties better handled by trained, certified teachers and that they might be having a negative impact on student achievement. The law prescribes the activities that paraprofessionals can lead and sets minimal requirements for their education and training.

Specifically, NCLB mandates that permissible paraprofessional responsibilities may include providing one-on-one tutoring for eligible students outside of classroom time, assisting with classroom management, organizing materials, assisting in a computer laboratory, conducting parental involvement activities, providing support in a media cen-

ter or library, or acting as a translator.[33] Under the law, new paraprofessionals must have obtained a high school degree; completed at least two years of study at an institution of higher education; obtained an associate's degree (or higher); or met a rigorous standard of quality and demonstrate, through a formal state or local academic assessment, knowledge of, and the ability to assist in instructing, reading, writing and mathematics, or reading readiness, writing readiness, and mathematics readiness, as appropriate.[34] Veteran paraprofessionals were given until the end of the 2005–2006 school year to meet the same requirements.

Charter Schools

The highly qualified teacher requirements pose a challenge for charter schooling. Charters are, in theory, supposed to enjoy greater flexibility in return for accountability; this includes the flexibility to hire teachers from nontraditional backgrounds. While most states exert some regulatory control over who teaches in charter schools, some states allow charters to hire uncertified teachers. In order to respect this while applying the highly qualified provision to all public schools, the authors of NCLB struck a compromise. NCLB stipulates that the bachelor's degree and subject matter requirements apply to charter schools just as they apply to traditional public schools. However, when it comes to certification, NCLB deferred to state law. It allowed each state to decide which certification requirements, if any, apply to charter school teachers. The significance of this provision should not be overstated. As the nonpartisan Education Commission of the States has reported, of the 39 states with charter school laws in 2003, only nine allowed charter schools to freely hire unlicensed teachers or apply for a waiver to do so. Thirty states required at least a portion of charter school teachers be certified, and 17 of those required full certification for all charter school teachers.[35]

The requirements present some challenges, especially for small charter high schools, where it is common for one teacher to instruct students in multiple subjects. Under NCLB, such a teacher either has to pass a test or have a major in each of those subjects or, if eligible, fulfill the state's HOUSSE procedures. The highly qualified teacher provision represents the most intrusive regulation that charter schools have faced, to date, from the federal government.

Alternate Routes to Teacher Certification

Congress also compromised with respect to teachers entering the profession from alternate routes to certification. These programs are often run by schools of education, seeking nontraditional candidates (like liberal arts graduates or mid-career professionals) and tailoring preparation to the particular needs of the candidates. They tend to "fast-track" candidates into the classroom, saving much of the training for on-the-job experience. The rationale for these alternate routes is many potentially highly qualified candidates will not pursue teaching if they cannot find a program that is convenient, inexpensive, and which acknowledges the value of their previous nonteaching experiences.

At first blush, NCLB seems to present significant obstacles for alternative route programs. Before the law, most of these programs provided an intensive training session the summer before the teacher candidate started teaching. The program administrators then worked with state officials to give the new teacher a provisional or emergency certification, while he or she completed the program's coursework at night or on the weekends over the following year or two. At the end of the process, the teacher would gain full state certification. Under NCLB, though, "highly qualified teachers" cannot hold provisional or emergency licenses.

Did NCLB's authors intend to eliminate such alternative certification programs? Clearly, they did not. In fact, the law explicitly mentions alternate routes as legitimate ways for a teacher to gain certification. Due to political compromises (and perhaps hasty drafting), the highly qualified teacher provision includes an internal contradiction: it supports alternate routes while outlawing the very mechanisms most states use to facilitate them.

The U.S. Department of Education attempted to address the resulting confusion through its regulations. Specifically, it declared that teachers participating in alternate certification programs could still be considered "highly qualified" as long as they:

1. receive high-quality professional development that is sustained, intensive, and classroom-focused in order to have a positive and lasting impact on classroom instruction before and while teaching;
2. participate in a program of intensive supervision that consists of structured guidance and regular ongoing support for teachers, or a teacher mentoring program;
3. assume functions as a teacher only for a specified period of time not to exceed three years; and
4. demonstrate satisfactory progress toward full certification as prescribed by the state.[36]

How this tension will ultimately play out and whether these measures will help states strike the intended balance remains to be seen.

What Must Districts and Schools Do?

Under NCLB's "Parent's Right to Know" clause, all districts that receive Title I funds must produce and disseminate an annual report card that includes accountability data and teacher quality information. The annual district report card must relate, for the district as a whole and for each school within the district: the professional qualifications of all teachers (bachelor's degrees, graduate degrees, licensure status, and so on) and the percentage of teachers with an emergency or provisional certificate. These report cards must be mailed to each parent in the district and made available to the local media. The report card requirement is designed to help parents judge school quality and to stimulate grassroots pressure for schools to hire qualified instructors.

Beyond the report cards, parents of students enrolled in Title I schools are entitled to additional information. Districts must notify these parents of their right to request information about their child's teacher, after which parents are free to request information on whether the teacher is licensed to teach the subject, whether the teacher is teaching with an emergency certificate, what field the teacher received his college major and/or certification in, and the qualifications of any paraprofessionals involved in their child's classroom.

If a class is taught for more than four weeks by a teacher who is not highly qualified, the district is required to notify the parents of each student in that class. This policy has proven controversial. Although veteran teachers supposedly had until 2006 to demonstrate that they were "highly qualified," any teacher who had not yet completed the process was to be labeled as not qualified in the letters to parents. Given that several states took years to design their HOUSSE systems, many local school districts saw this provision as unfair and simply refused to comply.

In order to produce and retain highly qualified teachers, the law encourages districts to improve recruiting by offering monetary incentives, reducing class size, implementing high-quality professional development, and/or developing new programs to improve teacher retention. How are districts to pay for this? Districts that receive Title I funding must dedicate 5% of this funding to teacher professional development and related activities. Districts are also allowed to spend additional Title I funds if the 5% allowance is not sufficient to make the required teacher quality improvements.

More significantly, NCLB created a separate funding stream for teacher quality activities. The Title II Teacher Quality State Grants program disbursed almost $3 billion to states and districts in 2005. Districts have considerable flexibility in how they spend this Title II funding. They can spend this money on professional development for teachers, bonuses, stipends, recruitment and retention incentives, or even to pay the fees for the state tests that new teachers must pass to demonstrate subject competency.[37] Because Title II was created by combining two pre-existing programs—President Clinton's Class Size Reduction program and the long-standing Eisenhower Professional Development program—Title II funds can also be used to pay for these activities. Despite their new flexibility, most districts continued to spend these dollars on class size reduction and professional development in math and science.

What Must States Do?

NCLB's highly qualified teacher provision is relatively broad, leaving the states to fill in the blanks. The law required states to create their own definition of a "highly qualified teacher," as well as devise a plan, complete with "annual measurable objectives," for producing such teachers. States were required to craft a set of rigorous teacher assessments for determining subject matter competency, create a HOUSSE system for their veteran teachers, and submit an annual progress report to the Secretary of Education. States are also expected to develop plans for addressing the teacher quality gap, explaining the mechanisms they will put in place to recruit and retain talented teachers in high-need schools.

Like districts, states must produce annual report cards that include information on teacher quality. The state report cards must include the same information as district report cards: the qualifications of all public school teachers (bachelor's degrees, advanced credits, teacher licenses), the percentage of teachers with provisional or emergency licenses, and the percentage of classrooms that are not staffed by a highly qualified teacher. These report cards must be made readily available to the public, typically via posting on the state Web site.

With regard to the specifics of producing and retaining such teachers, NCLB allowed each state to develop its own plan. Tennessee experimented with using consistent student achievement gains to determine whether teachers were highly qualified, seeking to link the status of teachers to the demonstrated achievement of their students.[38] Kansas and Iowa have made efforts to link their highly qualified academic standards to state university programs to ensure that all new teachers coming out of those universities will meet the requirements.[39] Oregon does not allow high school teachers to use HOUSSE provisions, and Alabama will not let any veteran teacher with fewer than 18 college credit hours in their specific content area use the state's HOUSSE provision.[40]

States receive Teacher Quality State Grant (Title II) funding to pay for statewide initiatives, though most of this money flows through to school districts. Allowable uses for this funding include reforming teacher licensure and certification systems, creating support and mentoring programs, providing professional development, and helping local school districts improve recruitment and hiring.

Federal Efforts to Help Schools and Districts

During the Bush administration's first term, Congress increased federal teacher quality aid dramatically, boosting it 35%, to almost $3 billion annually. The teacher quality state grants (Title II) are designed to help states and districts prepare, recruit, and hire highly qualified teachers.

To assist states in interpreting and implementing the highly qualified teacher requirements, former Secretary of Education Rod Paige formed the Teacher Assistance Corps (TAC). The TAC, made up of state and district officials, researchers, higher education leaders, and practitioners, helped states develop their definitions of a "highly qualified teacher" and their plans to help teachers meet the new standard.[41] The Department of Education also awarded a $35 million grant to the American Board for Certification of Teacher Excellence (ABCTE) in order to expand the organization's innovative alternative teacher certification system. ABCTE's Passport to Teaching program is designed for aspiring teachers that do not have the time, resources, or inclination to pursue a teacher credential through a traditional school of education. It seeks to ensure that aspiring teachers demonstrate professional and subject matter knowledge through a standard assessment. ABCTE was highlighted in former Secretary Paige's Second Annual Report on Teacher Quality as an approved provider of teacher certification under NCLB.[42] Critics have argued that ABCTE is an example of alternative certification intended to de-professionalize teaching. How widely states choose to adopt the Passport to Teaching and whether the ABCTE model works as intended remain open questions.

Flexibility in Implementation

The Department of Education has made several revisions to the highly qualified teacher provision in order to accommodate states, schools, and districts that were struggling with the requirements. The first change dealt with rural schools, which traditionally have difficulty finding qualified teachers. One rural superintendent explained: "This year, we hired two math teachers, but they had just been released by another school system. In both cases, they were virtually the only candidates. We hire and keep them for two to three years and then don't renew them. So we [rural districts] are passing around teachers who are not very competent."[43] Because teachers in small rural schools are often required to teach a number of different subjects, administrators have difficulty finding teachers highly qualified in each subject they are expected to teach.

Rural school proponents also argued that NCLB's AYP requirements could exacerbate the pressure on rural schools to find highly qualified teachers. Because rural schools often enroll large numbers of disadvantaged and ESL students, they are less likely to make AYP targets each year. When faced with a choice, new teachers or teachers looking to switch schools may be less willing to teach at a school that has been labeled "in need of improvement," putting the neediest rural schools at a disadvantage. As one rural school advocate put it in 2003, "They might be excellent teachers but could be branded a failure because certain students can't meet the standards."[44]

To alleviate some of the pressure on rural schools, in March 2004, former Secretary Paige announced a modification to the highly qualified teacher mandate for rural schools. Under the new policy, beginning teachers in rural school districts who are "highly qualified" in one subject now have three additional years to become highly qualified in the rest of the subjects that they teach. Veteran teachers will have an additional year to become highly qualified in their subjects. In order for districts to qualify for this flexibility, there are two requirements:

> First, the district must have fewer than 600 students in average daily attendance, or the district must be located in a county with fewer than 10 people per square mile. Second, all schools in the district must be located in communities with fewer than 2,500 residents.[45]

There are about 10,000 schools, enrolling nearly two million students, that are eligible for this flexibility; most are located in the Midwest and the Great Plains.[46]

This flexibility was particularly important to the many rural districts with large numbers of Native American or Hispanic students who live below the poverty line and speak English as a second language. Rural schools are often ill equipped to help these students make adequate yearly progress.[47] The increased flexibility allows schools to retain their current teaching staff while working to comply with the highly qualified teacher requirement. However, some districts have complained that the definition of "rural schools" is too strict, preventing most schools in the rural south, Appalachia, and rural New England from taking advantage of the policy.

Science Teachers and Teachers of Multiple Subjects

The U.S. Department of Education has also increased flexibility for science teachers and teachers of multiple subjects. School systems throughout the country suffer from a shortage of science teachers, a challenge particularly acute in urban and rural schools. In March 2004, the Department clarified its

policy, explaining that states have the option of allowing science teachers to demonstrate that they are highly qualified in the "broad field" of science rather than having to demonstrate it in particular fields such as chemistry, biology, or physics. Teachers certified in the "broad field" of science are able to teach multiple science classes rather than only the particular area in which their degree was earned.[48] In other words, a teacher who is certified in "broad field" science is qualified to teach biology, chemistry, and physics. Rural superintendents have expressed concern that there is no equivalent "broad field" certification for social studies teachers, who must still demonstrate competence separately in economics, history, civics, or geography to teach any of these courses.[49]

The last measure of flexibility granted by the Department of Education for groups with challenging circumstances extends to current teachers who teach multiple subjects. Rather than forcing these teachers to navigate the HOUSSE process for each of the subjects they currently teach, the Department has authorized states to "streamline this evaluation process by developing a method for current, multi-subject teachers to demonstrate through one process that they are highly qualified in each of their subjects."[50] There are few restrictions regarding how such a "streamlined" process must work, and the states are free to modify their HOUSSE procedure as they see fit. This policy could be especially relevant for special education teachers, who often instruct students in several core academic subjects.

State Flexibility

The Education Department has also shown some flexibility toward states that have taken creative approaches to fulfilling the HQT requirements. The most visible examples took place in Utah and North Dakota during 2004–2005. Both states sought to declare their veteran elementary teachers "highly qualified" based on their existing licensure regimes, believing that the state requirements were rigorous enough to satisfy NCLB subject matter competency requirements. Utah's HOUSSE standards for veteran elementary teachers essentially entailed a licensure-renewal process that requires teachers to have received positive professional evaluations and to have completed a college degree and district-run professional development courses. North Dakota did not set up HOUSSE standards for its existing elementary teachers, claiming that the existing licensure system ensured quality faculty.[51]

In late 2004, however, Department of Education officials voiced concerns that the Utah and North Dakota requirements did not fulfill NCLB's teacher quality mandate. The unofficial ruling set education officials in both states on edge, as an unfavorable decision could have cost federal funding or forced them to overhaul their existing teacher quality framework. After considerable political protest from state officials, the Department retreated and declared that veteran elementary teachers in both Utah and North Dakota would be considered highly qualified under the current state definitions, which included requirements regarding subject matter knowledge. The Education Department reportedly "never meant to imply that teachers in those states were not highly qualified—officials just needed to see documentation."[52] The Utah and North Dakota rulings could have implications for other states seeking additional flexibility in their HOUSSE procedures.

Are States on Track to Meet the HQT Requirements?

The Department of Education requires all 50 states and the District of Columbia to document the status of highly qualified teachers within its borders. Forty-three states turned in the report the first year, with twenty reporting that at least 90% of their classrooms statewide were already led by a highly qualified teacher.[53] According to Education Trust, these rosy findings need to be interpreted with "extreme caution." "A few states have been forthright with their data," a 2003 Education Trust report asserted, "but that some states have no data and most have questionable data reflects a shameful inattention to basic issues."[54]

Many states appear to be struggling to find teachers who are highly qualified and willing to work in their rural and urban areas. As Terry Moe and NCTQ have pointed out, many states have shaped their definition to make sure that most of their existing teachers are deemed highly qualified in order to avoid the expense and inconvenience of remediating under-qualified teachers or recruiting qualified ones. Other states make the initial certification process relatively easy for new teachers, at least when it comes to demonstrating subject matter knowledge. For example, as of 2004, fourteen states (Alabama, Alaska, Delaware, Idaho, Kansas, Maine, Montana, Nebraska, New Hampshire, New York, North Dakota, Rhode Island, Washington, and Wisconsin) did not test subject matter knowledge as part of recertification, and four more states (Iowa, South Dakota, Utah, and Wyoming) did not include a licensure assessment at all, in violation of the federal law.[55]

Consequences for States, Districts, and Teachers

One of the least discussed aspects of the highly qualified teacher provision relates to sanctions. What happens if a teacher is not highly qualified by 2006? What if a Title I school hires a new teacher who doesn't meet the standard? What if 10% or 20% of a state's teachers are not highly qualified by the deadline?

The short answer is that nobody yet knows. While Congress wrote detailed language regarding sanctions for low-performing schools under NCLB's accountability system (as described in chapter 2), the drafters of the law were virtually silent with respect to the consequences for failing to meet the highly qualified teacher provision. When it comes to non-Title I schools, at least, the law merely requires states and districts to have plans in place to meet the requirement and to demonstrate that progress is taking place on an annual basis. However, in its regulations, the U.S. Department of Education has decreed that districts would be "out of compliance" if they hired new teachers for Title I schools who were not highly qualified. The same would be true for districts with veteran teachers who were still not highly qualified after 2006. Nevertheless, the U.S. Department of Education has been careful from the beginning of implementation to explain that the law does not require teachers to be terminated if they fail to meet the law's standards. What exactly will happen to these teachers is a matter that states and districts will have to address.

States and districts have some additional time to resolve the issue. Secretary Spellings announced in October 2005 that states would be allowed to apply for a one-year extension to the "highly qualified teacher" deadline if they were showing "good faith" toward implementing its intent. Specifically, she explained that a state would get the extension if (1) it has a rigorous definition of a "highly qualified teacher"; (2) it does a good job of notifying parents of their teachers' qualifications; (3) the teacher quality data it reports to the federal government is accurate and complete; and (4) it takes aggressive action to ensure that poor and minority children have equitable access to experienced and qualified teachers.[56] Spellings appeared to be trying to use the carrot of additional flexibility to coerce states into embracing the spirit of the law. How effective this will prove remains to be seen.

Conclusion

No Child Left Behind's teacher quality provisions represent the most aggressive federal effort ever launched to address teacher quality. These requirements build upon the existent teacher quality focus of the Higher Education Act while expanding efforts to promote preparation and subject matter mastery.

In significant ways, the highly qualified teacher provision is at odds with much of the rest of NCLB. Most of the new elements of the law focus on the classic accountability bargain—setting clear standards for performance and clear consequences for failure, in

return for giving states, districts, and schools leeway as they go about producing the expected results. The highly qualified teacher provision, however, is an explicit effort to increase regulation of how schools and districts educate students. In pushing for new rules surrounding who is allowed to teach, Representative George Miller—the provision's Democratic champion—was essentially advancing the **opportunity to learn standards** promoted by the Clinton administration in the early 1990s while expressing his dismay with the teacher quality standard operating in most states.

Opportunity to learn standards

a 1990s education reform effort to define certain conditions for schools, districts, and states to meet so that all students would have the same opportunities for high-quality instruction and to justify educational expectations

The highly qualified teacher provision, for good or ill, fits awkwardly alongside NCLB's testing and accountability provisions. One can imagine the frustration of a rural school principal, for example, who is achieving impressive gains in assessed student performance but is forced to contend with state officials because her civics teacher majored in history. What matters more: student achievement or paper credentials? The law seems to want it both ways.

The result is statutory language and federal requirements that straddle the divide between proponents of extensive certification and critics of traditional licensure. By including full state certification in its definition of a highly qualified teacher, the highly qualified teacher provision has ratified, at the federal level, the traditional approach to teacher licensure. At the same time, the law's attention to alternate routes and its pressure for states to ensure that all teachers are credentialed could encourage states to experiment with new approaches. It is not yet clear how most states will resolve this tension or how these developments will alter the teaching landscape. Some states will likely pursue aggressive efforts to lower the bar required for highly qualified status; only time will tell how state efforts unfold. It appears that the provision will have a limited impact on the nation's veteran teachers, many of whom may be forced to endure a frustrating paperwork exercise, but most of whom will ultimately be labeled highly qualified.

Ultimately, the highly qualified teacher provision reflects the tension implicit in the relationship between the federal government and the states when it comes to education policy. NCLB presses states to establish detailed and rigorous systems for ensuring teacher quality and to do so in accord with federal directives, while trying to limit the explicit federal role. Whether this complex effort will yield a more effective teaching force is, at this point, an open question.

GLOSSARY

Core academic subjects—under NCLB, all teachers of the "core academic subjects" must be highly qualified. The core academic subjects are English, reading/language arts, mathematics, science, foreign languages, civics and government, economics, art, history, and geography.

Federal mandate—a command issued by the federal government requiring that private organizations, states, or local governments implement certain federal rules or decisions. In 1995, Congress enacted the Unfunded Mandates Reform Act to curb the federal government from issuing expensive, unfunded federal mandates. NCLB is generally not considered a federal mandate because states or districts can ignore its rules provided they decline federal education funding.

Federalism—is a form of government in which multiple levels of government have formal authority over the same land, area, and people. The United States was founded on the concept of federalism, splitting power among the federal government, individual states, and local authorities.

HOUSSE—is an acronym for the "high objective uniform state standard of evaluation." It is an important part of the highly qualified teacher definition. HOUSSE is used to assess an existing teacher's subject matter competency as an alternative to an examination, major, graduate degree, or advanced certification in the area being taught. States have great leeway to set HOUSSE standards.

Opportunity to learn standards—were an education reform effort from the early 1990s. The aim of the standards was to define a set of conditions by which schools, districts, and states had to abide to ensure all students had an equal opportunity to receive high-quality instruction so that students could meet educational expectations.

CHAPTER FOUR

Other Major Programs and Policies

Although No Child Left Behind's accountability, choice, and teacher quality provisions are the farthest-reaching elements of the law, they comprise only a small portion of the legislation's nearly 700 published pages. It is important to remember that the law encompasses ten separate titles authorizing more than 50 federal education programs as well as other important policies. This chapter focuses on two of the most significant changes to federal education policy brought by NCLB—the emphasis on education practices supported by "scientifically based research" and the muted attempt to provide greater flexibility and control to states and local districts. We will then consider one of the NCLB era's most contentious issues: federal education funding for the law. Finally, we close by briefly sketching the contours of other important programs in the statute.

Scientifically Based Research

Beyond No Child Left Behind's most sweeping changes—the introduction of results-based account-

ability and related choice provisions, and the requirement that all teachers be "highly qualified"—the
law includes a handful of other policies that also
signal fundamental change in the federal role in
education. The most important of these is the effort
to promote education practices supported by "scientifically based research." The phrase "scientifically based
research" appears more than 100 times throughout
the No Child Left Behind Act and is applied to policies addressing reading programs, teacher training,
drug prevention and school safety, and a range of other
topics. Scientifically based research has no title or program of its own, but it is woven into the fabric of virtually every program in the law. As a result, this
emphasis has potentially far-reaching consequences
for both daily classroom practice and academic
research related to education. In addition, by making the federal government a more active partner
in determining what specific instructional methods
should be approved for classroom use, NCLB also
sets a new precedent of federal involvement in curriculum and instruction. Eventually, this precedent
is likely to conflict with the long standing practice
of preventing the federal government from playing
any role in approving or dictating curricular materials.

What does the law mean when it talks about
scientifically based research? Box 1 gives the definition of scientifically based research included in
Section 9101.

More simply, scientifically based research means
research based on objective, empirical, systematic
observation that follows the scientific method. It
requires that studies employ scientifically valid, up-
to-date methodologies and analytical techniques
and that they pass muster with experts in the scientific community, preferably through publication in
peer-reviewed scientific journals.

So how is NCLB's focus on scientifically based
research a change for education policy, research,
and practice? First, with a clarity previously alien
to education, NCLB endorses the notion that virtually every aspect of what schools do should be

BOX 1: SCIENTIFICALLY BASED RESEARCH

Scientifically Based Research—

A   means research that involves the application of rigorous, systematic, and objective procedures to obtain reliable and valid knowledge relevant to education activities and programs; and

B   includes research that—

   i   employs systematic, empirical methods that draw on observation or experiment;

   ii   involves rigorous data analyses that are adequate to test the stated hypotheses and justify the general conclusions drawn;

   iii   relies on measurements or observational methods that provide reliable and valid data across evaluators and observers, across multiple measurements and observations, and across studies by the same or different investigators;

   iv   is evaluated using experimental or quasi-experimental designs in which individuals, entities, programs, or activities are assigned to different conditions and with appropriate controls to evaluate the effects of the assignment experiments, or other designs to the extent that those designs contain within-condition or across-condition controls;

   v   ensures that experimental studies are presented in sufficient detail and clarity to allow for replication or, at a minimum, offer the opportunity to build systematically on their findings; and

   vi   has been accepted by a peer-reviewed journal or approved by a panel of independent experts through a comparably rigorous, objective, and scientific review.

informed by scientific research. Historically, it has been accepted that educational practice would be based in large part on tradition, theory, and teachers' personal preferences.

NCLB also sets standards for the type of research that should be used to inform education practice. It establishes a "gold standard" for scientifically based research: the randomized, controlled study. A randomized, controlled study is a research technique that randomly assigns individuals to two different groups: a treatment group that receives the practice or intervention being studied and a control group that receives no treatment. Because the groups are randomly generated, there should be no relevant differences between them so long as they are of sufficient size. Consequently, a comparison of the results for the treatment group and the control group can allow researchers to see whether the treatment had any effect and to draw conclusions about the treatment's effectiveness. This is how most medical research into new drugs and treatments is conducted, and it is responsible for impressive advances in improving surgical techniques, developing preventive and therapeutic regimens, and combating conditions like heart disease and high blood pressure. Proponents argued that replicating this medical research model would yield similar benefits in education.

For example, if researchers want to examine whether a particular reading curriculum is effective for third graders, they might identify 100 similar schools willing to use the new approach and select by lottery the 50 that are to receive the treatment—in this case, the new curriculum. The other 50 schools—the control group—would continue to use their existing curriculum. The reading skills of all of the students would be assessed at the beginning of the experiment—before the new curriculum was introduced—and then at the end. Researchers would examine the progress of the students' reading skills to determine whether the new curriculum improved students' reading performance more effectively than existing practice.

Randomized-controlled studies

research designs that examine the effectiveness of a treatment by assigning individuals to two different groups, the treatment group and the control group

Although **randomized-controlled studies** are usually the most effective way to determine the effects of a particular curricular or instructional intervention, their ability to explain "how" an intervention works is limited. A randomized field trial of a reading program can reveal whether the program benefits participating students but may not shed light on why it helped or didn't help. Meanwhile, randomized field trials are not well suited for examining large, system-level interventions such as teacher tenure reform, site-based management, or the effects of the NCLB accountability apparatus. This is both because it is almost impossible to meet the controlled conditions required for a reliable randomized experiment and because the "treatments" cannot be readily isolated and applied, meaning that any outcomes are the product of complex interactions with the larger environment.

When randomized field trials are not practical or appropriate, quasi-experimental studies can provide a workable, second-best approach. These studies collect observational data about individuals receiving a variety of different treatments and use statistical methodologies to try to control for factors that might influence outcomes so as to tease out the effects of the different treatments.

While randomized-controlled studies are the norm in medicine and many branches of the sciences, the presumption that they are the most appropriate way to gauge the effectiveness of educational programs is relatively new and still controversial. While partisans on both sides of the major education debates of recent decades invoke research in debates about class size, teacher quality, reading instruction, and almost anything else, the research varies greatly in quality and relevance. Traditionally, appeals to "research" included everything from case studies to longitudinal surveys to randomized-controlled studies. These studies are not always equally valuable when making decisions about education policy and practice. Thus NCLB's scientifically based research provisions were intended not to require that all educational research adopt one particular methodological approach, but that educational practice be guided by research that is rigorous and reliable. Whether the implementation of the scientific research provision has struck a sensible balance between encouraging randomized field trials and respecting the utility of other forms of high-quality research, or whether the Institute for Educational Sciences at the U.S. Department of Education has been unduly focused on randomized experiments, has been a source of debate among educational researchers.

The push for scientifically based research is best illustrated by NCLB's Reading First program. Reading First marked a dramatic departure for federal policy, for it mandated a particular approach to the teaching of reading—one supported by decades of experimental and quasi-experimental research. Based on the conclusions reached by the National Reading Panel, convened in 1997 at Congress's request, the $1 billion per year Reading First program requires schools seeking funds to implement a comprehensive classroom-based reading program that includes the five elements of scientifically based early reading instruction: phonemic awareness (hearing and identifying individual sounds that make up spoken words), phonics (linking spoken sounds to written letters), fluency (ability to read accurately and quickly), vocabulary, and comprehension. The U.S. Department of Education's prescriptive Reading First approach caused great consternation among many state and local officials and book publishers. Critics have questioned the research underlying the Reading First effort and how the state applications are approved, and they have chafed at the federal government playing a more muscular role in curricular matters. Time will tell if this less flexible approach will result in increases in reading achievement.

There are many challenges implicit in promoting scientifically based methods, as exemplified by Reading First. For one, as stated earlier, it requires a major change in how educators and policy-makers make decisions. Many teachers have not been trained to evaluate or use research, nor is the school day structured to give teachers time to keep up with research developments. Furthermore, research studies do not always agree, and determining "what the research says" is not always straightforward. More fundamentally, beyond the area of early literacy, gold-standard randomized-controlled studies do not exist in most of the areas in which NCLB demands practices based on scientifically based research. In many cases, there are not even quality quasi-experimental studies.

To help sort through the existing studies and identify scientifically based research, the U.S. Department of Education launched the What Works Clearinghouse. The What Works Clearinghouse is intended to help educators understand which practices are supported by rigorous research and—just as importantly—which have been proven to be ineffective. The Clearinghouse is supposed to collect and screen studies on the effectiveness of educational programs, products, and practices; identify and review the studies with the strongest designs; and report on their strengths and weaknesses to inform educators and policy-makers on what the scientifically based evidence says about particular education issues. By holding up rigorous, gold-standard evaluations as the ideal, it also seeks to encourage researchers and developers of educational programs to engage in stronger research and evaluation, so that someday there will be a much larger body of practice supported by "scientifically based research." While lauded in concept, the initial design and execution of the Clearinghouse has been a subject of much dispute among scholars concerned that the standards for including studies were problematic or unevenly implemented.

Flexibility and Consolidation

Many early NCLB supporters were disappointed that the final law failed to do much to streamline and consolidate existing rules, regulations, and programs or provide states and school districts with more flexibility in using federal funds. Both the Bush administration's early blueprints for NCLB and the reform proposals floated by New Democrats had included plans to reduce paperwork and provide flexibility by consolidating small programs into broad funding streams, eliminating several smaller **competitive grant programs,** and shifting authority over education decisions back to the states and local districts. Only a few of these proposals actually became federal policy.

Why did the authors of NCLB believe flexibility and consolidation to be important? Education experts largely agree that schools function best when educators are given clear direction, held accountable for results, provided with the appropriate training and

Competitive grant programs

programs that require applicants to compete for limited federal funds support, and then given the autonomy to make decisions about how to teach and mentor their students. Federal education regulations that burden school and district officials with red tape or prohibit them from using resources in a fashion they deem appropriate can undermine school effectiveness. Giving local officials more freedom to allocate resources can help make federal education dollars more effective so long as flexibility is accompanied by accountability for student performance.

Policymakers believe consolidation is important because small programs can be inefficient. Small grant programs necessarily reach a limited number of schools and communities, have a limited impact, and often require districts to devote time and energy to seeking out funding and writing grant proposals. While most small competitive programs serve worthwhile purposes, it is necessary to consider the **opportunity costs** of these investments, or the benefits of alternative uses to which these resources might have been devoted. Small investments that partially attack a problem in a few communities might be more effectively combined with other resources to address a national priority.

By and large, the increased flexibility and consolidation sought by the more ambitious reformers in both the Clinton and Bush administrations were not reflected in the final law. Not only did almost all of the small discretionary programs targeted for elimination remain intact, but NCLB actually expanded the number of federal education programs.

NCLB did promote simplification in a few areas. For example, it consolidated a handful of formula and discretionary programs related to teacher quality, students with limited English proficiency, and education technology into three **formula grants.** The formulas more narrowly target these dollars to school districts with more disadvantaged children, while increasing the flexibility schools have to use the funds.

In addition, the law includes several provisions specifically intended to increase state and local flex-

Opportunity cost

an economic term defined as the use of a limited resource for one purpose that results in the loss of that resource for other uses

Formula grants/formula programs

these types of grants and programs provide funds to states or school districts automatically, based on certain formulas

ibility in spending federal aid. First, the law gives states and districts limited freedom to take federal aid targeted for one purpose and shift it to another. States may transfer up to half of the state share of funds for the Teacher Quality State Grant, Education Technology State Grant, Safe and Drug Free Schools, 21st Century Community Learning Centers, and Innovative Programs State Grant, to any other program in this list or to Title I. In practice, because most of the funding in these programs flows to local school districts, the amount of money that states may transfer is relatively small. At the local level, school districts may similarly transfer up to 50% of the funds they receive through these programs.

Second, NCLB creates a new State and Local Flexibility Demonstration project. This allows the Secretary of Education to enter into performance agreements with up to seven states and 80 local school districts to waive a variety of federal program requirements and allow them to transfer up to 100% of federal funds (other than Title I) to various programs and purposes. In exchange, the states and school districts entering into these agreements must set and meet educational performance goals.

Finally, NCLB includes specific provisions to increase the flexibility available to small, rural school districts. The amount of money these districts receive under federal formula grants is often too small to have an impact. NCLB enables the Secretary of Education to make grants to such school districts so that they can use these funds more effectively.

Why did the push to streamline federal education programs not go farther? The politics of consolidating and eliminating federal programs are complicated and quite tricky. Even the smallest program has an impassioned constituency of those who benefit from it and are willing to fiercely oppose any efforts to eliminate it. In addition, many programs also have "legislative champions," members of Congress who helped to create a program, who are committed to the particular issue it addresses, or whose district or state especially benefits from a particular program. The general public, on the other hand, is rarely aware of debates over the many small programs in question. As a result, there is political pressure to maintain existing programs and little political reward for reformers who attempt to weed out ineffective or low-priority programs.

The limited consolidation and flexibility measures of NCLB ultimately reflected a compromise. Prior to President Bush's 2000 election, most conservatives had championed an extreme form of consolidation. Touted as the "Straight A's" plan, it would have given any state or school district that wanted it broad flexibility to use funds from 14 different federal programs largely as they saw fit, in exchange for agreeing to meet multi-year student achievement goals. Critics argued that this approach amounted to a risky experiment with federal education funding. They also charged that it would have subjected states and school districts participating in Straight A's to less stringent accountability requirements than those adopted in NCLB and might reduce the **targeting** of federal funds on poor students. While rejecting the Straight A's approach, NCLB authorized the State and Local Flexibility Demonstration Project to generate evidence about how states and school districts use flexibility and where additional flexibility is needed. Few states or districts have shown interest in this pilot project, perhaps because it does not address their major concerns with NCLB—those around the AYP and highly qualified teacher provisions. In fact, as of 2005, only one state (Florida) and one district (Seattle) had obtained permission to exercise the pilot flexibility provision. Meanwhile, anecdotal reports suggest that districts are taking advantage of the "transferability" provision, which does not require prior approval or additional accountability.

No Child Left Behind includes one other important form of flexibility: "schoolwide" Title I programs. In the early decades of Title I, funds were targeted to needy students. These students were often pulled out of class for extra instruction. In

Targeting
the degree to which a federal education program's funding is focused on children living in poverty and on schools with high concentrations of students in poverty

recent years, policy-makers have been more interested in improving the entire school, rather than providing limited assistance to particular students. At first, only schools with very high percentages of low-income students could use their funds for such a "schoolwide" approach; the last several iterations of the Title I law have lowered this threshold and permitted more schools to do so. Now, under NCLB, more than half of all Title I schools operate "schoolwide" programs.

Funding

The pitch for NCLB presented a simple bargain to America's public schools: the federal government would demand more from them in accountability for student achievement but it would also provide them more flexibility and funding to help achieve this goal. The final version of NCLB did provide some additional flexibility, though not as much as some proponents and local educators had hoped. Likewise, the law was accompanied by increases in funding for education, though these were smaller than some had desired. Whether this funding has lived up to the promises of its proponents, and whether it is enough to help schools meet NCLB's goals, remains a subject of contentious debate.

Funding for the elementary and secondary education programs in NCLB did increase after the law's passage, rising nearly $8.9 billion, or 58%, between 2001 and 2004. The biggest beneficiary was Title I, whose annual funding increased by over $4 billion, or nearly half, during this time. Nonetheless, many Democratic legislators felt that funding increases following NCLB's passage did not live up to expectations set by the legislation and by President Bush. Indeed, by some calculations, the amount of federal funds appropriated by Congress for NCLB fell $36 billion short of the amount promised by the law through 2005.

How can funding for No Child Left Behind have increased so dramatically yet still leave schools and states disappointed? The answer is due, in part, in the complex process that determines annual federal spending. It can also be explained by the complexity of estimating about just how much NCLB actually costs. We will address each of these considerations in turn.

NCLB is a piece of "authorizing" legislation. It gives the federal Department of Education authority to carry out certain programs, spells out the rules that govern these programs, and gives Congress the authority to spend federal money on them. However, it does not actually provide any funding. This is done through the annual **appropriations** process.

Appropriation

the actual amount of money Congress decides to spend, or appropriate, on a certain program

Each year, Congress must pass, and the President must sign, 13 appropriations bills that make up the federal budget. Spending for programs in NCLB falls under a broader bill that includes annual funding for all Department of Education programs, as well as programs run by the Departments of Labor, Health and Human Services, and other related agencies. These annual appropriations bills actually determine how much the federal government spends on education.

When critics argue that NCLB is under-funded, what many are saying is that the funds appropriated by Congress in the annual appropriations bill are less than the maximum spending authorized. For example, NCLB authorized Congress to spend $20.5 billion on Title I in fiscal year 2005, but the actual appropriation was only $12.7 billion—a $7.8 billion difference. Note that such a discrepancy is not unusual. Appropriations bills, in almost every policy area, tend to provide significantly less spending than is authorized.

It is important to note that while NCLB programs are funded at less than what the law authorizes, neither authorized nor appropriated amounts necessarily have any relationship to what states and schools need to meet the law's goals and requirements. The authorized funding levels were set through a political bargaining process during NCLB's Congressional passage. They are not based on any kind of "scientific" estimate of the law's implementation costs, and they carry no assurance that the authorized amounts will be appropriated. It is possible that states and school districts did not need the entire $20.5 billion in 2005 to meet NCLB's goals. It is also possible that they actually required much more.

Several programs in No Child Left Behind are "under-funded" in the sense that annual appropriations are less than the amounts authorized by Congress. For the majority of programs authorized under No Child Left Behind, the legislation allows Congress to appropriate "such sums as may be necessary." Even so, Box 2 shows that a few major programs set specific maximum annual funding levels.

The appropriations process is controlled by Congressional appropriations committees, while the **authorization** process is driven by the Committee on Education and the Workforce in the House and the Health, Education, Labor, and Pensions Committee in the Senate. Legislators who set authorization caps are not the same as those who lead the appropriations process, and appropriators do not feel bound

Authorization
a piece of legislation that creates programs, sets rules, and spells out policies

BOX 2: "UNDER-FUNDING" OF NCLB			
Program	Authorized Funding (2005)	Appropriation (2005)	"Under-funding"
Title I	$20.5 billion	$12.74 billion	$7.76 billion
Twenty-First Century Community Learning Centers	$2 billion	$991 million	$1.01 billion
Innovative Programs State Grants	$525 million	$198.4 million	$326.6 million
FIE	$625 million	$580 million*	$45 million
Total for all programs	$23.65 billion	$14.51 billion	$9.55 billion

* includes funding for small discretionary programs authorized under FIE and earmarks.

by authorizations they did not set. Further, since authorizations don't actually guarantee that money will be spent, authorizing legislation is not constrained by requirements to restrain the growth of federal spending. Because appropriations do actually result in money being spent, appropriators are under both political pressure and Congressional rules to maintain government spending within certain limits. In Bush's first term, the costs of homeland security, the war in Iraq, and Medicare skyrocketed at the same time that tax cuts reduced government revenue, creating some pressure to limit domestic spending programs. Partly as a result, Congress and the President approved smaller appropriations for NCLB programs than were authorized, though the approved spending levels were still the highest in history.

How much does NCLB actually cost? The question is more complicated than simply looking at the funding authorizations, and there are no simple answers. NCLB requires states and school districts to develop additional tests to cover all grades where annual assessment is required, invest in technology and data management systems to keep track of AYP-related data, intervene in low-performing schools, and recruit and train highly qualified teachers. Even for the specific, concrete items on which NCLB requires states to spend additional funds, there is wide disagreement about what the costs are.

In 2002, the National Association of State Boards of Education (NASBE) estimated that implementing annual assessments as required by NCLB would cost states a combined $2.7 to $7 billion over seven years (somewhere between $386 million and $1 billion each year). The upper end of that range exceeded the amounts appropriated by Congress to help pay for states to implement the required assessments.[1] Shortly thereafter, a conservative-leaning group, AccountabilityWorks, estimated that implementing NCLB's annual testing requirements would cost states between $312 million and $388 million annually.[2] These separate analyses reached very different conclusions about the cost of testing because they are based on different assumptions and expectations about the kind of tests states should put in place. Accountability Works' estimates were based on the assumption that states would continue to use the type of tests many states already use: standardized multiple choice assessments that may be norm-referenced, rather than criterion-referenced, and that are not necessarily aligned to an individual state's standards. In contrast, NASBE's estimate presumed that each state would create new criterion-based assessments specifically aligned with its standards, incorporating free response and essay items (tests with such items are much more costly for states to grade than those that include only multiple choice items).

Government Accountability Office (GAO)

the investigative arm of Congress charged with examining matters relating to the receipt and payment of public funds

In 2003, the **Government Accountability Office (GAO)** conducted its own study of the implementation costs of the required NCLB assessments. It found that potential costs vary significantly depending on the quality of assessment used in a state and its estimates reflected this. GAO found the seven-year costs of implementing assessments would range from $1.9 billion for the least expensive tests, to $5.3 billion for the highest quality assessments, with $3.9 billion as the most likely estimate (or $557 million annually). In other words, the GAO study, generally regarded as unbiased and evidence-based, suggested that NCLB funds did cover the actual costs of the required assessments.[3]

Beyond the cost of assessments, however, the issue of how much NCLB costs becomes even murkier. For the most part, the law does not require states or districts to take specific actions or utilize specific inputs. Instead, the act's primary requirement is that schools produce academic results. This means that any discussion of how much the federal government "should" spend on NCLB programs raises two very tricky questions: How much do schools need to spend to ensure all children reach NCLB's proficiency goals? And who—states, the federal government, local school districts—should be responsible for paying the costs of reaching these goals?

Estimates as to how much it will cost states to comply with the entirety of NCLB have ranged to $100 billion or more.[4] Even if school finance experts could identify the precise amount of money each school in the country needs to ensure that all students meet the goals of NCLB, this still would not resolve the question of how much the federal government should spend on the law. After all, primary responsibility for education in this country remains with states and local communities, and all states have clauses in their constitutions requiring that they provide a thorough system of public education. If NCLB simply requires that states educate children to state-determined levels of proficiency, it's not clear whether it ought to be the responsibility of the federal government or the states to fund schools to the requisite level.

Ironically, NCLB itself may provide the tools necessary to solve some of these tricky questions. The law's annual testing, subgroup accountability, and proficiency requirements are generating an unprecedented wealth of information about which schools are and are not succeeding. The raft of student performance data can help researchers, policymakers, and educators better determine how much money schools need to provide an adequate education, what other structural and policy reforms are needed to enable them to do so, and what interventions are effective for particular student populations. These data might also arm funding equity advocates in their efforts to force states to spend more on education through lawsuits on behalf of poor districts.

Data generated by NCLB are likely to help advocates and state legislators make their funding systems more effective, but they cannot answer questions about how much the federal government *should* spend on No Child Left Behind. Ultimately, this is a political decision, to be resolved with one eye to the needs of states and communities working to meet NCLB's goals and the other on competing funding priorities and the extent of available resources.

All told, federal education spending remains quite limited relative to the expenditures by states and localities. Even with the large increases in federal spending under NCLB, federal funds accounted for less than 9% of all K-12 spending in 2005. If the law were funded at its fully authorized levels, as some Democrats have called for, this percentage would only be a few points higher. A reasonable question is whether the "tail" of education funding—the federal government—can continue to wag the "dog" of the entire education system without experiencing a serious backlash.

The Many Programs of NCLB

There are a variety of other programs in NCLB beyond those discussed so far. The vast majority of these existed prior to NCLB, having been enacted as part of the initial ESEA in 1965 or added in subsequent reauthorizations. They range from small programs of a few million dollars that fund a few grants to address specific issues (such as improving economic education or distributing free books to needy children) to multi-billion dollar grants distributed by formula to a majority of the nation's school districts. Any discussion of the programs in NCLB must start with a discussion of Title I.

Title I

Title I is the largest and most influential federal program funding K-12 education, and it focuses on improving education for disadvantaged students. Created in the initial ESEA of 1965, Title I is the bedrock of federal school efforts. Its funding, which totaled $12.7 billion in 2005, is distributed to all school districts in which **children in poverty** constitute at least 2% of school-age youth. Districts with higher concentrations of students in poverty receive more funding per pupil as the percentage of poor students increases. Fifty-eight percent of all public schools, and 96% of high-poverty public schools, receive Title I funds; a total of 14.9 million children receive Title I assistance.

Schools may use Title I funds for various activities intended to help improve achievement for disadvantaged students, including teacher professional

Children in poverty
children who live in homes in which the family income falls below the poverty line

development, hiring highly qualified teachers, improving the curriculum, extending learning time, offering after- or summer-school programs, providing additional supports for disadvantaged children (such as teacher aides or tutors), increasing parental involvement, and providing early childhood education. Schools where fewer than 40% of students are poor must use Title I funds only to help eligible disadvantaged children. Schools with more than 40% of students living in poverty may choose to operate "schoolwide programs" in which funding supports schoolwide improvement efforts that help both poor and non-poor students learn.

It is Title I spending to which NCLB's assessment and accountability provisions are tied. Some of the first sanctions to impact schools failing to meet NCLB performance goals require them to devote a percentage of Title I funds to certain purposes: 10% of Title I funds for teacher professional development and up to another 20% for providing supplemental educational services or transportation for public school choice. To be precise, the law requires districts to spend up to *an amount equal* to 20% of its Title I funds on transportation for public school choice and/or supplemental services, though it can use other federal, state or local funds for this purpose.

How did Title I change under No Child Left Behind?

The major changes to Title I were the ambitious efforts to strengthen accountability and provide options for students in low-performing schools. These were discussed at length in chapter 2. However, Congress also revised the formulas that allocate Title I funds in order to increase the share of funding directed to schools with the most disadvantaged students. In order to understand how this worked, it is necessary to understand that Title I funds are distributed through four separate formulas. The basic grant formula provides funds for every school district in which more than two percent of children live in poverty. This formula is based mainly on the relative number of poor children in the district, is weighted by state differences in educational spending, and ensures that some money flows to most of the nation's school districts. The second formula provides "concentration" grants on the same basis, but only to districts in which the number of poor children either exceeds 6,500 or is greater than 15% of the school-aged population. The third formula provides "targeted" grants to districts which teach a large percentage of poor children. Finally, the education finance incentive grants formula uses measures of state-level "equity" and "effort" to allocate aid and to encourage states to boost the amount of state spending and the equity of state funding formulas.

Prior to NCLB, the great majority of Title I funding flowed to school districts through the basic grants formula, which is the least targeted of the four. During the NCLB negotiations, legislators seeking to tighten the focus on serving disadvantaged students sought to add language requiring all increases in Title I funding (above the fiscal 2001 level) to be distributed through the "targeted" grants formula. While the Congressional appropriations committees have instead divided the increases evenly between "targeted" and "education finance incentive" grants, the result has nonetheless been greater targeting on needy districts.

NCLB included provisions to help state education agencies meet the new demands placed on them by the law's assessment and accountability requirements. To help cover these costs, Congress introduced state assessment grants to provide funds to help cover the costs of developing new standards and tests. NCLB even included a clause exempting states from annual testing requirements should Congress fail to fund this program. In 2005, the federal government provided $412 million in funding to help fund assessments. NCLB also included a new policy requiring states to devote at least 4% of their Title I funds to improvement efforts for the lowest performing schools.

Reading First

As explained earlier, Reading First is a new $1 billion program created by NCLB to help students in

Scientifically based reading research

a subcategory of scientifically based research, but the research here focuses specifically on reading

kindergarten through third grade learn to read by funding reading programs based on scientifically based research. Program funds pay for teacher training in evidence-based reading instruction and for instructional, diagnostic, and assessment materials. Any state may receive funds but only after showing it plans to use the aid in ways consistent with **scientifically based reading research.** States then award subgrants to disadvantaged school districts.

How did Reading First change under No Child Left Behind?

Reading First received much more funding under NCLB than had previous federal reading initiatives. The 2002 budget for Reading First was nearly $1 billion, four times the $250 million spent on the Reading Excellence Act the previous year. Reading First has also been implemented in a more hands-on manner, aided by the larger amount of funds available for technical assistance at the national level.

Teacher Quality Programs

Teacher Quality State Grants help states and local school districts recruit, hire, prepare, and retain highly qualified teachers. The federal government put almost $3 billion into the grants in 2005, with the money provided to states via a formula based on the size of the school-age population and the number of children living in poverty. States may use some of these funds to carry out statewide activities, such as reforming teacher licensure and certification systems, creating support and mentoring programs, providing professional development, and aiding local districts. However, most funds are distributed directly to school districts, which may use funds to improve teacher recruitment and retention, provide professional development, implement innovative approaches to improve teacher quality, and reduce class sizes.

How did the Teacher Quality Programs change under No Child Left Behind?

NCLB consolidated the class size reduction program and the Eisenhower professional development programs in order to create a single stream of funding intended to help states and school districts hire, recruit, retain, and develop highly qualified teachers. The change was designed to provide states and school districts greater flexibility in using federal funds, shift focus from class size reduction to improving teacher quality, and spark innovation. So far, however, there is little evidence that states or districts are using teacher quality funds in this manner. Many districts are still using federal teacher quality funds primarily to pay for additional teachers hired under the class size reduction program and to support professional development activities that had been initiated under the Eisenhower program.

NCLB also included two new teacher quality programs. The Math and Science Partnership program was designed to improve teacher content knowledge and skills in these subjects through a variety of training opportunities and through interactions with professionals and academics. The Transition to Teaching program provides funds to support the creation of new, alternative routes to teacher licensure so as to enable mid-career professionals from other fields to become teachers.

After-School and Technology Programs

In 2005, the twenty-first century community learning centers provided nearly $1 billion to states for after-school, summer, and weekend learning programs, particularly for low-income students in urban or rural areas. States distribute these funds to local school districts or community groups that run after-school programs.

How did after-school and technology programs change under No Child Left Behind?

The Twenty-First Century Community Learning Centers program was created in 1998 as a $40 million pilot project, with the Department of Education awarding small, competitive start-up grants to local after-school programs. By 2001 the program had grown to a national program that cost nearly $1 billion per year, and it was increasingly clear that the

U.S. Department of Education lacked the resources and staff to effectively monitor grantee quality. NCLB shifted responsibility for the program from the federal education department to the states. For the first time, NCLB also allowed community and faith-based organizations, such as the YMCA, to apply directly for after-school grants.

In 2005, education technology state grants provided almost $500 million to states and school districts to help them integrate technology into the curriculum and ensure that students master "twenty-first century" skills. The primary purpose of this program is to fund teacher professional development using technology. School districts that demonstrate they have solid professional development programs may also use funds for a range of technology-related purposes, including acquiring, developing, and maintaining computer hardware, software, and connectivity networks.

Education technology is one place in NCLB where the push for consolidation and flexibility prevailed. Before 2001, eight federal technology programs provided support for different technology-related activities. NCLB consolidated most of these programs into a single state formula program. As a result of this consolidation, federal education technology expenditures declined significantly, from $872 million across all eight programs in 2001 to just under $500 million for education technology state grants in 2005. The White House sought to eliminate these programs altogether in its 2006 budget. While these grants are unlikely to be eliminated by Congress anytime soon, the allocation will probably continue to remain level or decline for the foreseeable future.

English Language Learners

In 2005, the English language acquisition program provided more than $675 million to help schools educate students from non-English speaking backgrounds. School districts receive money through a formula based on the the size of their English language learner population and their population of immigrant children. Districts use funds both to help children learn English and also to ensure that English Language Learners are becoming proficient in core academic subjects.

How did the English language acquisition program change under No Child Left Behind?

Prior to NCLB, the federal government's investment in educating non-English speakers focused primarily on promoting bilingual education, an approach whereby children are taught mostly in their native language while slowly learning English. Funding was scattered among a number of competitive programs. There were two problems with this state of affairs. First, bilingual education had a poor track record; too many children from non-English speaking homes were not learning English. In the 1990s, these concerns led to a spate of state-level "English only" initiatives seeking to abolish bilingual education. Second, the number of students needing help with English has expanded dramatically—to more than 4.9 million children in 2003–2004—since these programs were created.[5] Many districts that had never before dealt with English language learners or immigrant students now were doing so. As a result, fragmented programs could not meet the needs of all the districts struggling to educate these students.

No Child Left Behind sought to address these problems by consolidating previous bilingual programs into a single-formula grant program focused on students' English language acquisition. In addition, NCLB required a limited English proficiency category in state accountability systems and required schools to show that students are learning English within three years of entering American public schools. To help districts meet these new expectations, Congress boosted funding for English Language Acquisition grants from $450 million for the various bilingual programs in 2001 to more than $675 million in 2005.

School Choice and Charter Schools

Because choice options for students in poorly performing schools play a key role in the law's accountability system, NCLB programs to support public school choices deserve attention. Before NCLB, the federal government's major choice-related efforts entailed supporting programs to provide seed money for charter schools and promoting racial integration by supporting magnet schools. NCLB expanded these efforts.

How did school choice and charter schools change under No Child Left Behind?

An amendment to NCLB sponsored by Senators Judd Gregg, the ranking Republican on the education committee, and Tom Carper, a Democrat from Delaware, created new programs to encourage public school choice and help charter schools pay for facilities. The Voluntary Public School Choice program provides incentives and funds for states and school districts to expand available choices. NCLB also authorized a program that provides competitive grants for organizations working to strengthen the financial position of charter schools so that they can more readily acquire facilities. A third provision of the Carper-Gregg legislation also addressed charter facilities. It set aside more than $200 million per year to provide matching grants to states that offer charter schools per-pupil funding for facilities. In 2005, more than $350 million in federal funds was appropriated to expand all forms of public school choice.

Safe and Drug-Free Schools

Safe and drug-free schools programs provide hundreds of millions of dollars for state and nationally supported activities to create and maintain drug-free, safe, orderly learning environments in and around schools. Collectively, the programs received more than $600 million in 2005. Of that amount, more than $400 million was distributed to states based on a set formula. The remainder was awarded directly by the federal government to nationally relevant school safety initiatives or to community and non-profit groups implementing proven programs.

Other Major Programs

The Fund for the Improvement of Education (FIE) allows the Secretary of Education to support, on a discretionary basis, smaller projects to improve elementary and secondary education. FIE has also become the authorization under which members of Congress insert special elementary and secondary education-related projects for their districts in annual appropriations legislation. Such projects are commonly known as "earmarks" or "pork." In the 2005 appropriations bill, Congress inserted 700 earmarks worth $245 million in FIE, leaving $12.1 million in discretionary funds for the secretary of education.

Impact aid, totaling more than $1.2 billion in 2005, provides financial help to districts which include large amounts of untaxed federal property. Such districts face unique financial challenges because they do not collect tax revenue from the federal land but must still educate the children living there. This situation arises with children living on military installations or on Indian land, in federally subsidized housing, or in similar circumstances. Impact aid aims to make up for the lost property tax revenue.

Conclusion

Amidst the heated debates over NCLB accountability, it is easy to forget that NCLB is not one program. Rather, it is an enormous, complex federal law that encompasses much of what the federal government does in the vast world of K-12 schooling. NCLB touches upon everything from school safety to grants for teacher quality to federal guidelines regarding educational research.

Ultimately, it's not clear how much the federal government is prepared to support these initiatives, how successful the various programs are, or how all of the moving pieces will fit together. Indeed, reflecting on the material we've covered thus far raises serious questions about policy implementation, political will, and the future of No Child Left Behind. It is to such questions that we now turn.

GLOSSARY

Appropriation—the actual amount of money that Congress decides to spend, or appropriate, on a certain program. In practice in the United States, the amount of money appropriated is typically less than the amount of money authorized.

Authorization—is a piece of legislation that creates programs, sets rules, and spells out policies. Within an authorizing statute, Congress often suggests a level of spending, but that number serves only as a ceiling. The actual amount to be spent is set by the Congressional "appropriation."

Children in poverty—children who live in homes in which the family income falls below the level established by the Department of Health and Human Services' poverty guidelines.

Competitive grant/program—type of grant and program requires applicants to compete with one another for limited federal funds, whereas "formula" grant programs automatically provide specified funding to eligible applicants. Grant applications are evaluated on quality, as well as other criteria included in the legislation, such as geographic distribution and the population served.

Formula grant/formula program—these types of grants and programs provide funds to states or school districts automatically, based on a formula that weighs factors such as poverty, population, number of children with certain special needs or conditions, and so on. The formulas differ from program to program. Some federal programs have both formula and competitive elements.

Government Accountability Office (GAO)—is the investigative arm of Congress charged with examining the implementation of federal programs.

Opportunity cost—an economic term defined as the use of a limited resource for one purpose that results in the loss of that resource for other uses.

Randomized-controlled study—is a research design that examines the effectiveness of a treatment or intervention by assigning individuals to two different groups: a "treatment group," which receives the intervention, and a "control" group, which does not. Researchers track results for both groups and compare them to determine the effect of the intervention.

Scientifically based reading research—is a subcategory of scientifically based research. However, the research focuses specifically on reading (see the glossary in chapter 1).

Targeting—is the degree to which a federal education program's funding is focused on schools with high concentrations of students living in poverty.

CHAPTER FIVE

Politics, Implementation, and Future Challenges

No Child Left Behind is very much a work in progress. In the years ahead, states will struggle to answer its challenges, and federal officials will try to ensure that the law is implemented as intended. The U.S. Department of Education is working with states while refining its own guidelines that spell out just what states, districts, and schools are expected to do. Moreover, NCLB itself will be up for reauthorization in 2007, allowing Congress to consider a range of radical alterations and more modest refinements.

Educators, parents, students, district officials, researchers, and involved citizens all have the opportunity to help inform and shape implementation and reauthorization. Any legislation that tackles a big, important, and emotionally charged issue like public education is inevitably going to get tangled in politics. How the public feels about the law and how state and federal officials work together will have as much to say about the prospects for NCLB as any efforts to address technical questions around assessment, AYP, or teacher quality. In this concluding chapter, we discuss how public opinion, state opposition, and federal maneuvering affect the prospects of NCLB. We will close by briefly considering the legacy of NCLB.

Public Opinion

Like most pieces of sweeping and compromise-filled legislation, NCLB elicits mixed reactions. Parents and voters tend to endorse its goals while voicing concerns about its means. Public knowledge of NCLB has grown incrementally since the law's adoption but nevertheless remains limited. In 2005, an Educational Testing Service (ETS) poll reported that the percentage of respondents aware of the NCLB reforms doubled from 2001 to 2005, but that even in 2005 just 61% had heard of the law.[1]

Annual *Phi Delta Kappan*/Gallup polling has documented a somewhat lower level of public familiarity with NCLB than has ETS polling. The 2005 *PDK*/Gallup poll reported that 59% of respondents said they knew little or nothing about the law—depicting a modest increase in public awareness from the 76% who said they knew little or nothing about the law in 2003. Even among the parents of public school students, in 2005, 54% said that they still knew little or nothing about the law.[2] In short, several years after the law's passage, it appeared that only half of adults knew enough about NCLB to have an opinion of the law.

How did people feel about the law after its first several years? On balance, public opinion is split and tugged by conflicting preferences. The ETS reported in 2005 that 45% of adults held a favorable view of NCLB and 38% held an unfavorable one, figures that were almost identical to the views of parents with children in school. Among those who had strong views, opinions were evenly split, with 19% of all adults holding a strongly favorable opinion and 21% a strongly unfavorable one. The ETS also reported what it termed a "worrisome . . . disconnect" between the views of adults on the one hand, and those of teachers on the other. While the general population had mixed feelings about the law, 75% of high school teachers viewed it unfavorably and just 19% viewed it favorably. Moreover, 50% of high school teachers held a strongly unfavorable opinion and just 2% held a strongly favorable one.[3]

A 2004 poll by the Public Education Network (PEN) found that the percentage of voters who favor the law declined slightly between 2003 and 2004, from 40% to 36%. During that time, the percentage of respondents opposed to the law increased from 8% in 2003 to 28% in 2004.[4] PDK/Gallup polling reported the most negative sentiment on NCLB, with the poll's authors concluding, "The NCLB strategies are frequently out of step with approaches favored by the public."[5] Though the survey did not ask a general "favorable/unfavorable" question, the PDK/Gallup effort found that 68% of respondents thought that student performance on a single test is not an adequate indicator of school success.[6] PDK/Gallup also reported that 80% of respondents felt that reading and math test results do not generate an adequate picture of school quality; that 82% thought basing school quality on reading and math tests will take attention away from art, music, and history; and that 79% said, if their child's school were identified as "in need of improvement," they would prefer having additional improvement efforts made within the school to transferring their child to a "non-needs improvement" school.[7] Such results suggest a lack of broad public support for many of the elements of NCLB. It is worth noting, though, that NCLB proponents have critiqued the relevance of the PDK/Gallup polling by making the case that the law does not rely on a "single test" and suggesting that the questions and findings of the PDK/Gallup poll are misleading and biased.[8]

Whatever the merits of the technical debate, the PDK/Gallup findings do reveal an important tension when it comes to the public's feelings about accountability. We have long known that the vast majority of adults endorse public school accountability in the abstract but are often uncomfortable with the specific testing provisions and sanctions required to put it into practice.[9]

The public's view of NCLB reflects these tensions. For instance, the Public Education Network has summarized its polling results by observing, "There is no doubt the American public wants public schools to be accountable for the performance of all students." At the same time, however, the PEN analysis noted, "While the public appreciates the light that NCLB shines on student performance, many are also concerned that the picture that is revealed is not always accurate. Nine of ten survey respondents said a single annual test cannot tell if individual students are performing satisfactorily, or if a school needs improvement."[10]

Americans are of two minds regarding the NCLB premise that all students and schools should be held to a uniform standard of achievement. On the one hand, the 2005 ETS poll found that 55% of adults and 59% of parents of school-aged children believe "all students, teachers and schools should be held to the same standard of performance," while just 34% of adults and 30% of parents disagree. At the same time, though, ETS also reported that just 26% of high school teachers believe in a uniform standard and that 60% reject such expectations.[11] Other surveys indicate that respondents are less supportive of race-based reporting and uniform standards than the ETS results may suggest. For instance, the 2005 *PDK*/Gallup poll reported that just 44% of respondents believe that test data should be disaggregated by race and that only 28% think special education students should be held to the same standard as their peers.[12]

The evidence also suggests that adults prefer to see school accountability based on student progress rather than on the absolute level of student achievement. The ETS reported in 2005 that adults preferred focusing on improvement rather than levels of achievement by 53% to 32%.[13] *PDK*/Gallup reported in 2005 that 85% preferred measuring school performance based on student improvement while just 13% preferred measuring it based on the percentage passing the state-mandated assessment.[14] These results suggest some public discomfort with the way AYP is currently calculated.

In a 2005 report, PEN coupled anecdotal evidence from nine public "hearings" on NCLB and survey results from an online poll of 12,000 respondents. Because both public meetings and online polls are nonscientific and tend to attract those with particularly strong feelings, these results should be treated with caution. Nonetheless, the outcomes may be instructive. The PEN report found overwhelming support for the goals of NCLB. Just one out of nine participants in the public meetings wanted to repeal the law, and only one out of four online respondents did. However, respondents voiced common concerns about standardized testing, with 9 of 10 saying that a single annual test is not a good indicator of whether a school needs improvement. Participants also expressed concerns that NCLB's labeling of schools as "in need of improvement" would create a stigma and lead the most engaged teachers and students to depart, or that it might lead parents and educators to blame certain groups of students for dragging down proficiency figures and causing school failure.[15]

In short, Americans feel about NCLB the way they feel about most far-reaching federal policies: they endorse the goals but are more skeptical about the details of the legislation. In the abstract, the public is supportive of efforts to hold educators accountable for student learning. When it comes to the practical realities of implementing NCLB, however, voters have been less enthusiastic—and surveys suggest that teachers have been quite critical. Nonetheless, while some popular press accounts about lawsuits, high-profile complaints, or state resistance paint a picture of widespread dissatisfaction, the reality is that public opinion several years after the passage of NCLB is still evolving. To the extent that members of the public have made up their minds, the results suggest a fuzzy picture that has morphed as NCLB implementation has proceeded.

State Resistance to NCLB

Press coverage has sometimes suggested that NCLB is widely unpopular. As we have seen from the public opinion data, however, the truth is that feelings about the law are very much mixed. The perception of widespread unpopularity has more to do with the attention devoted to the vocal resistance of some state and local governments than a clear shift in public sentiment. One year after the law's adoption, the Center on Education Policy reported, "States are generally committed to the goals of the No Child Left Behind Act and are trying hard to implement it."[16] As the costs and complexities of implementation have become clear, however, a growing number of state officials have expressed doubts about the law.

In 2004, lawmakers in 31 states proposed legislation that either sought greater flexibility on implementation or called for limiting state participation in NCLB.[17] The criticism has come from both sides of the aisle in statehouses and in the U.S. Congress. In Oklahoma, for example, a resolution brought by state Democrats in 2004 calling on Congress to overhaul the law was shelved in favor of another resolution—championed by a conservative Republican—that favored repealing NCLB entirely. Republican legislators in Arizona and Minnesota introduced bills that would allow those states to reject some provisions of NCLB. Vermont voted to prohibit the use of state funds for NCLB-related programs while, in Utah, the Republican-controlled House refused to implement parts of NCLB for which it did not receive adequate federal funding.[18] School districts in various states have sought to opt out of NCLB by forfeiting the attached federal funds, and a handful of districts have actually done so. Meanwhile, the National Education Association (NEA) and the state of Connecticut are among those who have backed lawsuits that challenge the law's legality. (The NEA's

lawsuit was thrown out by a federal judge in November 2005 but litigation continues in various forms.) Republican Arlen Specter, chairman of the Education Subcommittee of the Senate Appropriations Committee, observed in March 2005 that, "The pot is definitely boiling on this law. The law is good on standards and accountability, but it clearly needs some modifications, because it's going through growing pains."[19]

State resistance has ranged from some states grumbling and requesting Department of Education waivers to a few states actively threatening to forfeit their federal aid and opt out of the NCLB system. In the first few years under NCLB, Vermont, Colorado, and Utah were among the states where legislative challenges to the law were fiercest. In Vermont, legislators considered a bill that would preclude the state from complying with any of NCLB's requirements. Colorado's state senate considered a law that would have allowed districts to ignore NCLB requirements and seek tax increases to compensate for lost federal funding. A North Dakota proposal would have prohibited the state from imposing sanctions on schools or districts which chose to ignore NCLB.[20]

Some of the most aggressive and outspoken state opposition to NCLB has come from an unlikely source: the state of Utah, a staunchly conservative state that provided President Bush with his largest electoral margin in the 2004 election. Utah Republicans voiced anger at federal intrusiveness and demanded freedom from NCLB strictures on testing and on reporting achievement data. "It chains us," said one Republican representative and school teacher. "It's an intrusion that I'm baffled by," said another.[21] In 2004, led by Republican representative Margaret Dayton, the Utah statehouse attempted to pass a bill that would opt the state out of NCLB. The effort attracted national attention, a problem for an administration in the middle of an election year. The bill almost passed. It was defeated only after high-ranking Department of Education officials and White House staff visited the state and told lawmakers that opting out of NCLB would cost them $106 million in federal funding. According to one representative, "They tried to strong-arm us. They tried to undermine our opposition with threats of lost revenue."[22] Though the "posse" dispatched from Washington successfully derailed the 2004 effort, Utah lawmakers were far from finished.

In early 2005, Dayton again rallied Republican legislators to challenge the Department of Education in what *Education Week* termed a "nationally watched showdown."[23] Dayton put forward a modified plan that was eventually signed into law by the Republican governor. The new plan exempted local school districts from implementing NCLB-related activities that are not paid for by federal funding. If a Utah district uses this state law to refuse to implement parts of NCLB, it will be instructive to see the U.S. Department of Education's reaction. State and local policymakers around the nation are watching closely.

The Federal Response

In responding to state resistance, the Bush administration has employed two, sometimes conflicting, approaches. On the one hand, U.S. Department of Education officials have repeatedly reaffirmed their commitment to NCLB's accountability goals and their insistence that states and school districts abide by the spirit of the law. On the other hand, Department officials have made some modifications to the law's regulations and granted some states increased flexibility. The goal has been to give states enough leeway so that none will simply opt out of the law and walk away from their federal education funding, while still encouraging states to conform to the NCLB template as closely as possible. As the Secretary of Education has negotiated this tension, some critics have accused the Department of being too willing to compromise while others have accused it of being inflexible. Meanwhile, critics of all stripes have complained about a lack of transparency in the Department's decision making process.

The Department of Education has mostly stuck

to its guns when defending NCLB, often dismissing or downplaying state resistance. As an administration spokesperson said in spring 2005, "One hundred or so superintendents and a handful of state resolutions, only a few of which have actually passed both houses, hardly qualify as a widespread rebellion. No one should be surprised, and we certainly aren't, that there is some anxiety about change. It's a sign the law is working."[24] Similarly, former Secretary of Education Rod Paige told a reporter in early 2004, "For every person out there who is criticizing this law, there are tens of thousands out there who are supporting it."[25]

While offering this staunch rhetoric, however, the Department has modified several of NCLB's most unpopular provisions and offered states flexibility on a variety of fronts, including some of the most important accountability and teacher quality provisions. In fact, in 2004, Paige told educators that the Department was trying to "wring every ounce of flexibility out of the [law's] existing language."[26]

In late 2003, the Department announced changes that would grant schools more flexibility in meeting the testing requirements for students with disabilities. Under the new arrangement, students with serious disabilities would be tested using "alternative assessments," and up to 1% of a school's population, or 10% of its special education students, would be exempted from AYP calculations. Shortly thereafter, in early 2004, Paige announced that limited English proficiency (LEP) students would be granted a one-year transition period during their first year in an American public school; the test scores of just-arrived immigrants would not count against a school. One month later, the Department announced changes to NCLB's highly qualified teacher mandate that included relaxed requirements and timelines for rural teachers, teachers of multiple subjects, and science teachers. In late March 2004, Paige announced that the strict rules governing student participation in testing had been softened to allow schools to average their rates over three years to achieve the required 95% standard.[27]

The Bush administration brought in a new Secretary of Education after its victory in November 2004, and states hoped that Margaret Spellings, a close advisor to the President, might be more flexible than outgoing Secretary Rod Paige. Indeed, the early stages of Secretary Spellings's tenure suggested a determination to couple a rhetorical defense with a willingness to offer substantially more flexibility to states than the administration had countenanced in the law's initial years. During her Senate confirmation hearings, Spellings signaled her likely course by explaining that she was committed to implementing NCLB in a "sensible and workable" manner. She elaborated on this statement in an interview shortly after her confirmation, asserting that there was "room to maneuver" within NCLB's existing language while cautioning, "I don't want people to think that No Child Left Behind is up for grabs."[28]

In April 2005, Spellings announced that a larger percentage of students with disabilities (especially those with learning disabilities) could be exempted from the regular state tests. On the highly qualified teacher provision, both North Dakota and Utah successfully pressed the Department to reverse an earlier decision and declare both states' veteran certified teachers "highly qualified." Some observers attributed the reversal to the political pressure applied by both states' congressional delegations, though the Department insisted it had simply needed additional documentation to grant approval.[29]

Spellings also acquiesced in part to the request of California's Republican governor, celebrity Arnold Schwarzenegger, that his state be allowed to modify its accountability system so that districts would only be labeled as "in need of improvement" if students from the same subgroup failed to reach proficiency in consecutive years.[30] This meant that if a school's Latino subgroup missed AYP one year but made it the following year, while its low-income subgroup made it the first year but missed in the second year, the school would no longer be identified as "in need of improvement." Some observers were surprised at the quick response of the Department in this case, when states such as Utah and Texas had been told to be patient. In another example of Department flexibility, Missouri successfully lobbied the Department to permit the state to adjust downward the Missouri proficiency targets for "communication arts" and math for 2004–2005.[31]

Perhaps the most significant example of a state receiving special treatment in Secretary Spellings's early tenure emerged in Florida, where the President's brother, Jeb Bush, was a second-term governor. Florida asked the U.S. Department of Education for permission to exclude the achievement of subgroups from the AYP calculation for individual schools unless a group constituted at least 15% of the school's population or included at least 100 students. The U.S. Department of Education agreed to Florida's request. In practice, the decision means that whether a middle school with 800 students that enrolls 80 African-American students, 70 Hispanic students, and 60 special needs students "makes AYP" will no longer depend on each of these subgroups clearing the Florida AYP bar. Rather, these students will only affect the school's AYP performance so far as they affect the school's overall proficiency level. Political and media elites in Florida welcomed the Department's decision as demonstrating sensible flexibility, while minority advocates and defenders of special needs students were alarmed that the change would make it easy for schools to overlook their most vulnerable students.

Yet another Department action that attracted notice was Spellings's decision in the fall of 2005 to allow four districts to alter the sequence of the NCLB remedies by offering supplemental services after year two and public choice only after year three. This decision raised eyebrows, given that it appeared to violate the law's explicit language. A slightly less controversial Spellings decision was her fall 2005 decision to grant waivers to some urban districts that had failed to make AYP so that they could nonetheless continue to provide supplemental services. While the waivers did not contradict the letter of the law, they did contradict the rules on supplemental service that Department had issued just a few years earlier. Yet another hotly debated decision was the Secretary's October 2005 announcement that the deadline for meeting the "highly qualified teachers" requirement would be postponed a year for those states which could demonstrate that they were making a good-faith effort.

As of January 2006, the most important concession made by Secretary Spellings may have been her November 2005 announcement that up to 10 states would be allowed to alter their accountability systems so as to track the progress of students over time. This pilot program sought to address one of the key criticisms of NCLB: that it punishes schools whose students are making remarkable progress but who start the school year at such a low level of performance that they are unlikely to reach the state's proficiency bar. Education interest groups reacted favorably to this decision, with the National Education Association declaring it "a step in the right direction."[32] Advocates for NCLB were not as sure, however, with Education Trust's Kati Haycock sounding a cautionary note: "We had so-called growth models before NCLB, and they did little to drive reform or improvements for students. The question we can answer with a good pilot is whether a new generation of growth-based accountability systems will do more to drive the necessary changes in teaching and learning than the current model."[33]

As these decisions make clear, federal officials are forced to walk a fine line between allowing states to eviscerate the law and being so inflexible that states rebel. Given the politics of Washington, DC, the decision of just two or three states to abandon the law could be seen as a major embarrassment for the administration and an invitation to mass rebellion. Moreover, should a few states opt out, their senators and members of Congress would become major impediments for efforts to expand, fund, or even sustain NCLB. Consequently, the administration has been left to play a delicate game of "chicken" with the states, trying to give in just enough to maintain their cooperation without compromising the essence of the law. How successfully the Bush administration's Department of Education walks that line, and whether future administrations will manage the trick, will do much to determine the fate of NCLB.

What Is Ahead for NCLB?

Viewed through one lens, NCLB promotes educational accountability and parental choice policies long championed by conservative reformers. Seen from another angle, it marks a radical break with conservative tradition, initiating a massive shift of education authority from states to Washington, the sort of thing more characteristic of "big government" Democrats than laissez-faire Republicans. The law's far-reaching provisions will powerfully influence how schooling is delivered across America. Indeed, in many ways, NCLB recalls the towering promises, ornate implementation challenges, and dashed hopes of President Lyndon Johnson's Great Society, a legacy that initiated the Elementary and Secondary Education Act and also fueled the conservative ascendance that would carry George Bush to the presidency.

Today, more than a half century after the famous desegregation case of *Brown v. the Topeka Board of Education,* in which the U.S. Supreme Court issued a unanimous decision outlawing racial segregation in America's schools, observers see a job only half done. As Howard Fuller, chairman of the board of the Black Alliance for Educational Options argued on the case's fiftieth anniversary, "The *Brown* decision sent a powerful message by tearing down the legal structures of oppression, but there remains plenty of unfinished business."[34] Many of NCLB's strongest proponents see the law's purpose as helping to finish that job. First Lady Laura Bush told a conference of the National School Boards Association, "At the time of *Brown v. [Topeka] Board of Education,* some people thought black children didn't deserve to be in the same classroom as white children. . . . Now today, there are still some people who believe some children can't achieve high standards. No Child Left Behind is based on the premise that all children must have access to high quality schools regardless of their skin color, their disability, or their zip code."[35]

In championing NCLB, the Bush administration took up the surprising role of advocating ambitious new federal policies and programs in education. Reversing mid-1990s Republican efforts to dismantle the U.S. Department of Education, the Bush White House instead crafted an elaborate new regulatory regime forcing states and communities to help fulfill the educational promises President Johnson made in the 1960s. The administration wrapped its actions in the mantle of racial and social justice, arguing federal intervention was needed to protect poor and minority children from neglect and local interests. Today, as was the case forty years ago, a well-meaning President has striven to use his moral authority—decrying "the soft bigotry of low expectations"—first to prod the Congress, then to press state and local officials to ignore self-interest and long standing arrangements. At times, while defending the law and urging the states forward, the administration has been so enchanted by its grand aspirations that it has sometimes seemed oblivious to the realities of human nature, organizational behavior, and the complications that ensue when implementing ambitious federal laws. The irony, of course, is that for more than three decades this was the defining conservative critique of the Great Society.

The Bush administration's commitment to equal educational opportunity and the difficulties of fulfilling that promise may remind the historically inclined of the Eisenhower administration's bold rhetoric justifying federal intervention in the *Brown* decision. While generally unenthusiastic about federal activity, Eisenhower deemed federal leadership essential to ensuring black children the educational opportunities promised by *Brown*. We should remember, however, that the Eisenhower administration

found appeals to justice—even those backed by a unanimous Supreme Court—insufficient. Ultimately, the Eisenhower administration had to deploy the National Guard just to get black children through the schoolhouse door. In demanding deep, complex changes across tens of thousands of schools, NCLB sets a course that is even more ambitious and yet brings far less muscle to bear.

No Child Left Behind asks state and local officials to undertake tasks that many regard as unnatural, unrealistic, or at odds with their self-interest. Moreover, the "street level bureaucrats" who share primary responsibility for NCLB's success are public school educators who enjoy abiding credibility with parents and voters. Opposition from these educators could undermine the law's promise to "leave no child behind," and it is not clear that federal officials know how to answer such a challenge. Nobody expects the National Guard to administer tests or mount tutoring programs. Federal officials cannot force states to fulfill the "spirit of the law," much less ensure that educators in 15,000 school districts or 85,000 schools will do so. The Department of Education has rarely even withheld federal dollars in order to punish states that fail to comply with federal requirements, a refusal that many NCLB proponents pointed to when explaining why states never adopted the accountability measures that the 1994 ESEA reauthorization "required" them to adopt.

Given NCLB's sweeping goals and awkward construction, winning and sustaining the support of critical constituencies will require moral authority that rewards cooperation and makes resistance politically unpalatable. Achieving this goal will require support from Democratic as well as Republican leaders. A law as big and ambitious as NCLB is unlikely to last if it is seen as a partisan bill, especially given the prickly relationships between the two major teachers unions and the Republican leadership. In the end, it seems likely that the fate of NCLB will rest in large part on how future Democratic administrations, Congressional leaders, and state officials view the law. Whether NCLB will receive their backing in the years ahead is an open question.

Political support is only the beginning. Federal statutes seldom succeed in changing behavior through good intentions or powerful rhetoric. When they work, it is generally because they are sensibly designed, understood by citizens and voters, and effectively use mandates and incentives in a measured fashion. Scholars in the 1960s and 1970s explained the surprisingly disappointing results of widely heralded Great Society programs by recognizing that Washington's money and direction are often no match for real-world complexities. Will No Child Left Behind turn out to be another such sobering lesson, or a case of federal law making a dramatic difference for tens of millions of America's children? The answer is not yet clear. Forty years after the unsatisfying results of the Elementary and Secondary Education Act and fifty years after the unfulfilled promise of *Brown,* a bipartisan coalition crafted a law designed to honor our common dreams for America's children. Whether their monumental effort will come to fruition, we will have to determine, together, in the years ahead.

Appendix
The Many Programs of NCLB

The No Child Left Behind Act authorizes more than 50 federal education programs, some new and some that existed previously. The following chart lists the programs, the section of the bill in which they can be found, and their 2005 authorization and funding levels.

Program Name[156]	Sec.	Purpose	Type	2005 Funding (2005 authorization)
Title I	I(A)	Improve education for disadvantaged children	Formula grant to LEA	$12.74 billion ($20.5 billion)
Reading First	I(B)1	Support scientifically based reading programs in grades K-3	Formula grant to State	$1.04 billion
Early Reading First	I(B)2	Support scientifically based early literacy programs for preschoolers	Competitive Grant to local applicants	$104 million
Even Start	I(B)3	Promote early education and adult literacy in low-income families	State grants	$225 million
Improving Literacy Through School Libraries	I(B)4	Support school library materials, media, and training	Competitive Grant to LEA[157]	$19.7 million
State Agency Programs	I(C)	Improve education and coordination for migratory children and for neglected, delinquent, and at-risk children, including those in institutions or public care	Formula grant to State	$440 million
Comprehensive School Reform	I(F)	Encourage comprehensive school reforms	Formula grant to State	$205 million
Advanced Placement	I(G)	Expand AP classes, pay test fees for disadvantaged students	Formula grant to States	$29.8 million
School Drop-out Prevention	I(H)	Prevent school drop-out and facilitate re-entry	Competitive grant to states and LEAs[158]	$4.9 million

Program Name[159]	Sec.	Purpose	Type	2005 Funding (2005 authorization)
School Improvement[160]	Sec. 1003(g)	Improve schools identified under NCLB	Formula grant to states	$0
Teacher Quality State Grants[161]	II(A)	Help and hold states and LEAs accountable for having a highly qualified teacher in every classroom	Formula grant to States	$2.9 billion
Math and Science Partnerships	II(B)	Improve teacher content knowledge in science and math	Competitive grants to partnerships	$178.6 million
Transition to Teaching	II(C)1	Establish programs for mid-career professionals to become teachers	Competitive grants	$44.9 million
National Writing Project	II(C)2	Teacher professional development in the teaching of writing	Secretarial award to National Writing Project	$20.3 million
Civic Education	II(C)3	Support "We the People" and international education exchange programs	Secretarial award to Center for Civic Education and National Council on Economic Education	$29.4 million
Teaching of Traditional American History	II(C)4	Encourage teaching of history as a separate subject	Competitive grants to LEA	$119 million
Teacher Quality National Activities	II(A)5 Sec 2151	Support National Teacher Quality Initiatives or Projects. Currently includes: preschool educator professional development (e), advanced credentialing (c), and school leadership (b)	Chosen by Secretary or Congress	$46.4 million for 3 initiatives
Education Technology	II(D)1	Support technology in K-12 schools	Formula grant to States	$496 million

Program Name	Sec.	Purpose	Type	2005 Funding (2005 authorization)
English Language Acquisition[6]	III(A)1	Improve education and language acquisition for non-English speaking children	Formula grant to States	$675.8 million
Safe and Drug Free Schools	IV(A)	Support programs to prevent violence and illegal use of tobacco, alcohol, and drugs by students and in or around schools	Formula grant to LEAs	$437.4 million
Safe and Drug Free Schools National Activities	IV(A)2	Support nationally significant drug and violence prevention programs, including alcohol abuse reduction and mentoring	Secretarial awards	$234.6 million
21st Century Community Learning Centers	IV(B)	Support after-school programs	Formula grant to States	$991 million ($2 billion)
Innovative Program Grants	V(A)1	Support state and local education reform	Formula grant to LEAs	$198.4 million ($525 million)
Charter School Programs	V(B)1	Support creation and implementation of charter schools and encourage state charter school efforts[7]	Grant to States	$217 million
Credit Enhancement for Charter School Facilities[8]	V(B)2	Demonstrative innovative credit enhancement initiatives that help charter schools with the cost of acquiring or improving facilities	Competitive grants	$37 million
Voluntary Public School Choice	V(B)3	Support inter- and intra-district public school choice programs	Competitive grants to States and LEAs	$26.5 million

Program Name	Sec.	Purpose	Type	2005 Funding (2005 authorization)
Magnet School Assistance	V(C)	Encourage magnet schools to support public school choice and desegregation.	Grants to LEAs	$107.8 million
Fund for the Improvement of Education	V(D)	Allow Secretary to support nationally significant programs. This section also specifically authorizes several programs: • Elementary and Secondary school counseling ($34.7 million) • Character Education ($24.5 million) • Reading Is Fundamental ($25.3 million) • Javitz Gifted and Talented ($11 million) • Star Schools ($20.8 million) • Ready to Teach ($14.3 million) • Foreign Language Assistance ($17.9 million) • Physical Education ($73.4 million) • Community Technology Centers ($4.96 million) • Exchanges with Historic Whaling and Trading Partners ($8.6 million) • Excellence in Economic Education ($1.5 million) • Improving Mental Health ($4.96 million) • Foundations for Learning Grants ($992,000) • Arts in Education ($35.6 million) • Parental Information and Assistance Centers ($41.9 million) • Combating Domestic Violence (Not funded) • Healthy, High Performance High Schools (Not funded) Women's Educational Equity Act ($2.96 million)	Secretarial award: grants, contracts, or cooperative agreements	$257 million $323.4 million appropriated for specified programs Total: $580 million ($625 million)

Program Name	Sec.	Purpose	Type	2005 Funding (2005 authorization)
Enhanced Assessment Instruments	*VI(A)1 Sec 6112*	*Fund state assessments required under Title I*	*Formula grants to States*	*$311.7 million*
Rural Education	*VI(B)*	*Address needs of rural communities that receive small allotments in formula programs*	*Grants to States*	*$170.6 million*
National Assessment of Educational Progress	VI(C) Sec. 602	Establish a regular national assessment of student achievement in reading, math, and other subjects	Funds National Assessment Governing Board	$94 million
Education for Native Hawaiians	VII(B)	Develop innovative educational programs to assist Native Hawaiians, and encourage Native Hawaiian participation	Secretarial awards: grants or contracts	$34.2 million
Alaska Native Educational Equity	VII(C)	Improve education of Alaska Native students, support Alaska Native cultural and language education	Secretarial awards: grants or contracts	$34.2 million
Indian Education	VII(A)	Support efforts to meet unique educational and culturally related needs of American Indian and Alaska Native students	Formula grants to LEAs and Tribes. Secretarial awards (grants or contracts) for special projects and national activities	$119.9 million
Impact Aid	VIII	Compensate school districts that lose revenue or incur expenses due to federal land ownership or high concentration of federally dependent children	Formula to LEAs	$1.24 billion

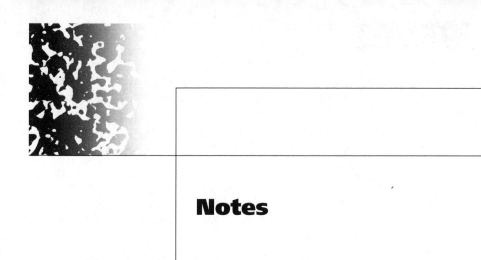

Notes

Chapter One

1. Office of the White House Press Secretary, "Press Release: President Signs Landmark Education Bill," January 8, 2002.

2. Andrew Rudalevige, "No Child Left Behind," in *No Child Left Behind? The Politics and Practice of School Accountability*, eds. Paul E. Peterson and Martin R. West (Washington, DC: Brookings Institution Press, 2003): 23–24.

3. John Kerry, "The Promise of Opportunity," *Phi Delta Kappan*, 86, no. 2 (2004): electronic archive.

4. Lorraine M. McDonnell, "No Child Left Behind and the Federal Role in Education: Evolution or Revolution?" *Peabody Journal of Education* 80, no. 2 (2005): 19–38.

5. Nel Noddings, "Rethinking a Bad Law," *Education Week*, February 24, 2005.

6. Lawrence A. Uzzell, "No Child Left Behind: The Dangers of Centralized Education Policy" (Washington, DC: Cato Institute: Washington, DC May 3, 2005): 1.

7. Margaret Spellings, "Our High Schools Need Help . . ." *Washington Post*. April 2, 2005: A21.

8. Robert Gordon, "Class Struggle," *The New Republic*. June 6, 2005.

9. Ross Wiener, "In Virginia, Reopening the Gap," *Washington Post,* June 6, 2005: A19.

10. Public Papers of the Presidents of the United States, *U.S. Government Printing Office 1965*, Lyndon B. Johnson, Book I (1963–1964): 704–707.

11. Julia Hanna, "The Elementary and Secondary Education Act: 40 Years Later," *Ed. Harvard Graduate School of Education* (Summer 2005): 6–13, p. 8.

12. Diane Ravitch, "A Historical Perspective on a Historic Piece of Legislation," in *Within Our Reach: How America Can Educate Every Child,* ed. John Chubb (New York: Rowman & Littlefield, 2005): 35–51.

13. Frederick M. Hess and Patrick J. McGuinn, "Seeking the Mantle of 'Opportunity': Presidential Politics and the Educational Metaphor, 1964–2000," *Educational Policy* 16, no. 1 (2002): 72–95.

14. Hess and McGuinn, 2002.

15. Ravitch, 2005: 35–51.

16. Hanna, 2005: 13.

17. Statement of Richard W. Riley, Secretary of Education, before the U.S. House of Representatives Committee on Education and the Workforce on the Reauthorization of the Elementary and Secondary Education Act of 1965. February 11, 1999.

18. Al Gore, commencement address at Graceland College, Lamoni, Iowa, May 16, 1999.

19. Initial draft of No Child Left Behind submitted by the White House, 2001.

20. Siobhan Gorman, "Bipartisan Schoolmates," *Education Next* 2, no. 2 (2002): 36–43.

21. Initial draft of No Child Left Behind submitted by the White House, 2001.

22. Gorman, 2002.

23. Chester E. Finn, Jr., and Frederick M. Hess, "On Leaving No Child Behind," *The Public Interest* 157 (2004): 35–56.

24. Abigail Thernstrom and Stephen Thernstrom, *No Excuses: Closing the Racial Gap in Learning* (New York: Simon and Schuster, 2003).

25. "Forum: Do We Need to Repair the Monument?" *Education Next* 5, no. 2 (2005): 9–19.

26. Michelle Melendez and Martha Deller, "Bush Education Plan Gets Mixed Response," *Fort Worth Star-Telegram.* January 28, 2001: 1.

27. Richard F. Elmore, "Unwarranted Intrusion," *Education Next* 2, no. 1 (2002): 31–35.

28. Finn and Hess, 2004; Thomas J. Kane, Douglas O. Staiger, and Jeffrey Geppert, "Randomly Accountable," *Education Next* 2, no. 1 (2002): 56–61; Robert L. Linn, "Accountability Models," in *Redesigning Accountability,* eds. Susan Fuhrman and Richard Elmore (New York: Teachers College Press, 2004): 73–93.

29. W. James Popham, *America's "Failing" Schools: How Parents and Teachers Can Cope with No Child Left Behind* (New York: Routledge, 2005).

30. Richard Rothstein, *Class and Schools: Using Social, Economic, and Educational Reform to Close the Black-White Achievement Gap* (Washington, DC: Economic Policy Institute, 2004).

31. Alfie Kohn, "NCLB and the Effort to Privatize Public Education," in *Many Children Left Behind: How the No Child Left Behind Act Is Damaging Our Children and Our Schools,* eds. Deborah Meier and George Wood (Boston: Beacon Press, 2004): 79–97.

32. Richard F. Elmore, "Unwarranted Intrusion," *Education Next* 2, no. 1 (2002): 31–35.

Chapter Two

1. David W. Grissmer, Ann Flanagan, Jennifer Kawata, and Stephanie Williamson, *Improving Student Achievement: What State NAEP Test Scores Tell Us* (Santa Monica, CA: Rand Corporation, 2000).

2. President George W. Bush, "President Discusses No Child Left Behind and High School Initiatives," J.E.B Stuart High School, Falls Church, VA: January 12, 2005. Available at www.white-house.gov/news/releases/2005/01/20050112–5. html

3. Education Commission of the States, *ECS Report to the Nation 2004* (Denver, CO: Education Commission of the States, 2004): 23.

4. For a collection of anti-NCLB essays, see Deborah Meier and George Wood, eds., *Many Children Left Behind: How the No Child Left Behind Act Is Damaging Our Children and Our Schools* (Boston: Beacon Press, 2004).

5. George Wood, "Introduction," in *Many Children Left Behind: How the No Child Left Behind Act Is Damaging Our Children and Our Schools,* eds. Deborah Meier and George Wood (Boston: Beacon Press, 2004): vii-xv.

6. Linda Darling-Hammond, "From 'Separate but Equal' to

'No Child Left Behind': The Collision of New Standards and Old Inequalities," in *Many Children Left Behind: How the No Child Left Behind Act Is Damaging Our Children and Our Schools*, eds. Deborah Meier and George Wood (Boston: Beacon Press, 2004): 9.

7. See Robert Linn, "Rethinking the No Child Left Behind Accountability System" (Boulder, CO: National Center for Research on Evaluation, Standards, and Student Testing, 2004).

8. U.S. Department of Education, "Key Policy Letters Signed by the Education Secretary or Deputy Secretary" (Washington, DC: U.S. Department of Education, November 2005). Available online at http://www.ed.gov/policy/elsec/guid/secletter/051121.html

9. Jacquelyn C. Jackson, "Policy Guidance: Use of Title I Funds, Districts and Schools in Need of Improvement" (Washington, DC: U.S. Department of Education, October 12, 2004).

10. Richard Lee Colvin, "Public School Choice: An Overview," in *Leaving No Child Behind? Options for Kids in Failing Schools*, eds. Frederick M. Hess and Chester E. Finn, Jr. (New York: Palgrave Macmillan, 2004): 11–36.

11. Robert Maranto and April Gresham Maranto, "Options for Low-Income Students: Evidence from the States," in *Leaving No Child Behind? Options for Kids in Failing Schools*, eds. Frederick M. Hess and Chester E. Finn, Jr. (New York: Palgrave Macmillan): 63–89.

12. Colvin, 2004: 13.

13. Citizens' Commission on Civil Rights, "Choosing Better Schools: A Report on Student Transfers Under the No Child Left Behind Act" (Washington, DC: Citizens' Commission on Civil Rights, May 2004).

14. Citizens' Commission on Civil Rights, 2004: 7.

15. Erik Robelen, "Guidance Urges Input on Dangerous Schools Definition," *Education Week* 23, no. 39 (2004): 31.

16. Thomas L. Good and Jennifer S. Braden, *The Great School Debate: Choice, Vouchers, and Charters* (Mahwah, NJ: Lawrence Erlbaum, 2000).

17. Siobhan Gorman, "The Invisible Hand of NCLB," in *Leaving No Child Behind? Options for Kids in Failing Schools*, eds. Frederick M. Hess and Chester E. Finn, Jr. (New York: Palgrave Macmillan, 2004): 37–61.

18. Frederick M. Hess and Chester E. Finn, Jr., *Leaving No Child Behind? Options for Kids in Failing Schools* (New York: Palgrave Macmillan, 2004): 290.

19. U.S. Department of Education, Office of the Deputy Secretary, Policy and Program Studies Service, *Case Studies of Supplemental Services Under the No Child Left Behind Act: Findings from 2003–04.* (Washington, DC, 2005) vi.

20. See Hess and Finn, "Conclusion," 286–303.

21. Hassel and Steiner, 2003.

22. Loveless, 2003.

23. Gary Miron and Brooks Applegate, "An Analysis of Edison Schools Opened in 1995–96," The Evaluation Center, Western Michigan University (Kalamazoo, MI: The Evaluation Center, 2000). Henry Levin, "Thoughts on For-Profit Schools," *Education Matters* 1, no. 1 (2001): 6–15.

24. Education Commission of the States, "Policy Brief: State Takeovers and Reconstitutions" (Denver: Education Commission of the States, March 2004); Kenneth Wong and Francis X. Shen, "City and State Takeover as a Reform Strategy" (Washington, DC: ERIC Clearinghouse on Urban Education, July 2002).

25. Education Commission of the States, 2004.

26. Education Commission of the States, 2004.

27. Center for Education Policy, "Hope but No Miracle Cures: Michigan's Early Restructuring Lessons" (Washington, DC: Center on Education Policy, November 2005).

Chapter Three

1. Sandra Huang, Yun Yi, and Kati Haycock, *Interpret with Caution: The First State Title II Reports on the Quality of Teacher Preparation* (Washington, DC: The Education Trust, June 2002): 3. Available online at www2.edtrust.org/NR/rdonlyres/305751B5–7635–4F5E-9BBE-068CF0849150/0/titleII.pdf.

2. Vivian Troen and Katherine C. Boles, *Who's Teaching Your Children? Why the Teacher Crisis Is Worse Than You Think and What Can Be Done About It* (New Haven: Yale University, 2003): 46.

3. U.S. Department of Education, "The Seven Priorities of the United States Department of Education—Working Document" (Washington, DC: U.S. Department of Education, 1997). Available online at www.ed.gov/updates/7priorities/7prior.pdf.

4. U.S. Department of Education Office of Postsecondary Education, *Highly Qualified Teachers Challenge: The Secretary's Annual Report on Teacher Quality* (Washington, DC: U.S. Department of Education, 2002): 4.

5. Dan Goldhaber, "Why Do We License Teachers," in *A Qualified Teacher in Every Classroom: Appraising Old Answers and New Ideas,* eds. Frederick M. Hess, Andrew J. Rotherham, and Kate Walsh (Cambridge, MA: Harvard University Press, 2004): 91.

6. Kate Walsh, "Teacher Certification Reconsidered: Stumbling Toward Quality" (Baltimore: The Abell Foundation, 2001): 6.

7. See Walsh, 2001: 5–8.

8. June C. Rivers and William L. Sanders, "Teacher Quality and Equity in Educational Opportunity: Findings and Policy Implications," in *Teacher Quality,* eds. Lance T. Izumi and Williamson M. Evers (Palo Alto, CA: Hoover Institution Press, 2002).

9. Goldhaber, 2004: 92.

10. Michael B. Allen, *Eight Questions on Teacher Preparation: What Does the Research Say?* (Denver, CO: Education Commission of the States, 2003).

11. See David Angus, *Professionalism and the Public Good: A Brief History of Teacher Certification* (Washington, DC: The Thomas B. Fordham Foundation, 2001).

12. Andrew Rotherham and Sara Mead, "Back to the Future: The History and Politics of State Teacher Licensure and Certification," in *A Qualified Teacher in Every Classroom: Appraising Old Answers and New Ideas,* eds. Frederick M. Hess, Andrew J. Rotherham, and Kate Walsh (Cambridge, MA: Harvard University Press, 2004).

13. C. Emily Feistritzer, *Alternative Teacher Certifications: A State by State Analysis* (Washington, DC: National Center for Alternative Certification, 2005).

14. The Education Trust, "Not Good Enough: A Content Analysis of Teacher Licensing Examinations," *Thinking K-16*, 3 no. 1: 7–8.

15. Rotherham and Mead, 2004: 26.

16. Frederick M. Hess, "The Predictable, but Unpredictably Personal, Politics of Teacher Licensure," *Journal of Teacher Education* 56 no. 3: 192–198.

17. Rotherham and Mead, 2004: 44.

18. See Heidi Ramirez, "The Shift from Hands-Off: The Federal Role in Supporting and Defining Teacher Quality," in *A Qualified Teacher in Every Classroom: Appraising Old Answers and New Ideas,* eds. Frederick M. Hess, Andrew J. Rotherham, and Kate Walsh (Cambridge, MA: Harvard University Press, 2004): 49–79.

19. Ramirez, 2004: 60.

20. National Commission on Teaching and America's Future, "What Matters Most: Teaching for America's Future" (New York: National Commission on Teaching and America's Future, 1996).

21. Ramirez, 2004: 66–67.

22. Huang, Yi, and Haycock, 2002: 4.

23. Huang, Yi, and Haycock, 2002: 1.

24. National Association of State Directors of Teacher Education and Certification, *The NASDTEC Manual on the Preparation & Certification of Educational Personnel*, 2001: G-6.

25. Kate Walsh and Emma Snyder, "Searching the Attic: How States Are Responding to the Nation's Goal of Placing a Highly Qualified Teacher in Every Classroom" (Washington, DC: National Council on Teacher Quality, 2004).

26. The New Jersey Model for Identifying Highly Qualified Teachers, *The New Jersey HOUSE Standard: Content Knowledge Matrix*. Available online at www.state.nj.us/njded/profdev/ hqt/house.pdf.

27. Walsh and Snyder, 2004: 2.

28. Terry Moe, "The Qualified Teacher Charade," *Hoover Institution Weekly Essays* (Stanford, CA: The Hoover Institution, October 2004): 2.

29. Moe, 2004: 2.

30. Christopher O. Tracy and Kate Walsh, "Necessary and Insufficient: Resisting a Full Measure of Teacher Quality" (Washington, DC: National Council on Teacher Quality, Spring 2004).

31. Tracy and Walsh, 2004.

32. Walsh and Snyder, 2004.

33. No Child Left Behind Act. Part A. Subpart 1. Sec. 1119. Qualifications for Teachers and Paraprofessionals (g) (2) (A-F).

34. No Child Left Behind Act. Part A. Subpart 1. Sec. 1119. (c.) New Paraprofessionals (1) (A-C (ii)).

35. Education Commission of the States, "Charter Schools and the Teaching Quality Provisions of No Child Left Behind" (Denver: Education Commission of the States, 2003).

36. U.S. Department of Education Academic Improvement and Teacher Quality Programs, *Improving Teacher Quality State Grants Title II, Part A: Non-Regulatory Guidance* (Washington, DC: U.S. Department of Education, 2004): 10.

37. U.S. Department of Education Academic Improvement and Teacher Quality Programs, *Improving Teacher Quality State Grants Title II, Part A: Non-Regulatory Guidance* (Washington, DC: U.S. Department of Education, 2004): 33–35.

38. Bess Keller, "Snapshot of 'Highly Qualified' Teachers Is Fuzzy," *Education Week* 23, no. 2 (2003): 24, 28.

39. U.S. Department of Education, "Press Release: Charting the Course: States Decide Major Provisions Under No Child Left Behind" (Washington, DC: U.S. Department of Education, January 2004). Available online at www.ed.gov/news/press-releases/2004/01/01143004.html#qualified.

40. Tracy and Walsh, 2004: 9.

41. United States Department of Education. *No Child Left Behind: A Toolkit for Teachers* (May 2004): 12.

42. American Board for Certification of Teacher Excellence, "American Board Receives $35 Million in Federal Funding" (Washington, DC: Education Leaders Council and National Council on Teacher Quality, Sept. 25, 2003).

43. Quoted in The Southeast Center for Teaching Quality, "NCLB Teaching Quality Mandates: Findings and Themes from the Field" (Chapel Hill, NC: Southeast Center for Teaching Quality, March 2004): 2.

44. Quoted in Courtney Cobb, "No Child Left Behind Act Hurts Rural Schools, Say Education Experts," *Idaho State Journal,* online edition, December 12, 2003.

45. Robin Lambert and Marty Strange, "The Rural School and Community Trust Fact Sheet" (Washington, DC: The Rural and Community Trust, 2003): 1. Available online at www.ruraledu.org/issues/nclb/HQT_Flex_factsheet.pdf.

46. Lambert and Strange, 2003.

47. Cobb, 2003.

48. *No Child Left Behind: A Toolkit for Teachers* (Washington, DC: U.S. Department of Education, 2004).

49. Erik Robelen, "Federal Rules for Teachers Are Relaxed," *Education Week* 23, no. 28 (2004): 1, 30–31.

50. *No Child Left Behind: A Toolkit for Teachers*, 2004.

51. Bess Keller, "N.D., Utah Dispute Federal Findings on Teacher Quality," *Education Week* 24, no. 18 (2005): 5.

52. Linda Jacobson, "Federal Officials Say N.D., Utah Teachers 'Qualified' After All," *Education Week* 24, no. 26 (2005): 20.

53. The Education Trust, *Telling the Whole Truth (or Not) About Highly Qualified Teachers* (Washington, DC: The Education Trust, December 2003): 4.

54. Education Trust, 2003: 1, 4.

55. Education Trust, 2003: 6.

56. U.S. Department of Education, "Key Policy Letters Signed by the Education Secretary or Deputy Secretary" (Washington, DC: U.S. Department of Education, October 2005). Available online at http://www.ed.gov/policy/elsec/guid/secletter/051021.html.

57. National Association of State Boards of Education, "Press Release: Costs of President's Testing Mandate Estimated as High as $7 billion." Available online at www.nasbe.org/archives/cost.html.

58. Theodore Rebarber and Thomson W. MacFarland, "Estimated Cost of the Testing Requirements Under the No Child Left Behind Act," Paper for Education Leaders Council Test Summit, AccountabilityWorks, 2002. Available online at www.schoolreport.com/AWNCLBTestingCostsStudy.pdf.

Chapter Four

1. General Accounting Office, "Characteristics of Tests Will Influence Expenses; Information Sharing May Help States Realize Efficiencies" (Washington, DC: General Accounting Office, May 2003).

2. William J. Mathis, "The Cost of Implementing the Federal No Child Left Behind Act: Different Assumptions, Different Answers," *Peabody Journal of Education* 80, no. 2 (2005): 90–119.

3. The National Clearinghouse for English Language Acquisition and Language Instruction Educational Programs, May 2005.

Chapter Five

1. Peter D. Hart and David Winston, *Ready for the Real World? Americans Speak on High School Reform* (Washington, DC: Educational Testing Service, 2005).

2. Lowell C. Rose and Alec M. Gallup, "The 37th Annual Phi Delta Kappa/Gallup Poll of the Public's Attitudes Toward the Public Schools," *Phi Delta Kappan*, September 2005: 49.

3. Hart and Winston, 2005.

4. Public Education Network, *Learn. Vote. Act.: The Public's Responsibility for Public Education* (Washington, DC: Public Education Network, 2004).

5. Rose and Gallup, September 2005: 43.

6. Rose and Gallup, 2005: 50.

7. Rose and Gallup, 2005: 50.

8. Terry M. Moe, "Cooking the Questions?," *Education Next* 2, no. 1 (2002): 70–77.

9. Frederick M. Hess, "Refining or Retreating? High Stakes Accountability in the States," in *No Child Left Behind? The Politics and Practice of School Accountability*, eds. Paul E. Peterson and Martin R. West (Washington, DC: Brookings Institution Press, 2003).

10. Public Education Network, *Open to the Public: Speaking Out on "No Child Left Behind"* (Washington, DC: Public Education Network, 2005): 4, 17–19.

11. Hart and Winston, 2005.

12. Rose and Gallup, 2005: 51.

13. Hart and Winston, 2005.

14. Rose and Gallup, 2005: 52.

15. Public Education Network, 2005.

16. Center on Education Policy, *From the Capital to the Classroom: State and Federal Efforts to Implement the No Child Left Behind Act* (Washington, DC: Center on Education Policy, 2003): 1.

17. The reference to 31 states is attributed to the National Conference of State Legislatures—see Lynn Olson, "States Revive Efforts to Coax NCLB Changes: Some Legislators Seek Waivers Under Law," *Education Week* 24, no. 21 (2005): 1, 29.

18. Michael Dobbs, "More States Are Fighting 'No Child Left Behind' Law," *Washington Post*, February 19, 2003: A3.

19. Specter quoted in Sam Dillon, "President's Initiative to Shake Up Education Is Facing Protests," *The New York Times*, March 8, 2004: 12.

20. Olson, 2005: 29.

21. Davis, 2005: 21.

22. Davis, 2005: 21.

23. Michelle Davis, "Utah Is Unlikely Fly in Bush's Ointment," *Education Week* 24, no. 22 (2005): 1, 21.

24. Susan Aspey quoted in Dillon, March 8, 2004.

25. Dobbs, 2004: A3.

26. Sam Dillon, "U.S. Set to Ease Some Provisions of School Law," *The New York Times*, March 14, 2004: 1.

27. Press releases outlining the four changes can be found at: http://www.ed.gov/news/pressreleases/2004/07/index.html?src =ln.

28. Quoted in Erik Robelen and Lynn Olson, "Spellings to Listen, but Not Retreat, on NCLB," *Education Week* 24, no. 22 (2005): 5.

29. Linda Jacobsen, "Federal Officials Say N.D., Utah Teachers are 'Qualified' After All," *Education Week* 24, no. 26 (2005): 20.

30. George Archibald, "Arnold Wields Clout on Education Issues," *Washington Times*, March 23, 2005: A5.

31. Olson, 2005: 29.

32. National Education Association, "NCLB 'Growth Model' Plan Called Step in Right Direction" (Washington, DC: NEA, November 2005). Available online at: http://www.nea.org/ esea/growthmodel.html.

33. Education Trust, "Education Trust Statement on U.S. Department of Education's Announcement of a Growth-Model Pilot Program" (Washington, DC: Education Trust, November 2005). Available online at: http://www2.edtrust.org/EdTrust/ Press+Room/growthmodel.htm.

34. Howard Fuller, "The Struggle Continues," *Education Next* 4, no. 4 (2004): 27–29, p. 29.

35. Mike Schneider, "First Lady Offers Support, Paige Offers Changes to Education Law," The Associated Press State & Local Wire, March 29, 2004.

Appendix

1. Programs in italics are new in NCLB.

2. If funding exceeds $100 million, this program becomes a formula grant to states.

3. For funding that is less than $75 million. For funding between $75 and $250 million, competitive grants for states, funding greater than $250 million, formula to states with competitive subgrants to locals.

4. This is new to ESEA legislation. The Clinton administration had previously established "Title I accountability" funds for school improvement through the budget process.

5. This consolidated funds from the Eisenhower Professional Development Grants that previously existed under ESEA and Class Size Reduction program established during the Clinton Administration.

6. This was consolidated and refocused from previously exist-

ing bilingual education programs.

7. If funding exceeds \$200 million, the excess will support per-pupil facilities aid programs for charter schools.

8. Funds were appropriated for this purpose in the 2001 budget, but authorizing legislation was not passed in ESEA prior to NCLB.

Peter Lang PRIMERS

in Education

Peter Lang Primers are designed to provide a brief and concise introduction or supplement to specific topics in education. Although sophisticated in content, these primers are written in an accessible style, making them perfect for undergraduate and graduate classroom use. Each volume includes a glossary of key terms and a References and Resources section.

Other published and forthcoming volumes cover such topics as:

- Standards
- Popular Culture
- Critical Pedagogy
- Literacy
- Higher Education
- John Dewey
- Feminist Theory and Education
- Studying Urban Youth Culture

- Multiculturalism through Postformalism
- Creative Problem Solving
- Teaching the Holocaust
- Piaget and Education
- Deleuze and Education
- Foucault and Education

Look for more Peter Lang Primers to be published soon. To order other volumes, please contact our Customer Service Department:

       800-770-LANG (within the US)
       212-647-7706 (outside the US)
       212-647-7707 (fax)

To find out more about this and other Peter Lang book series, or to browse a full list of education titles, please visit our website:

       www.peterlangusa.com